Christians, Beware
The Dangers of Secular Psychology

By
Magna Parks, Ph.D.

Carol Roberts
Wildwood College
435 Lifestyle Lane.
Georgia

TEACH Services, Inc.
Brushton, New York

2007 08 09 10 11 12 · 5 4 3 2 1

Copyright © 2007 TEACH Services, Inc.
ISBN-13: 978-1-57258-511-9
ISBN-10: 1-57258-511-0
Library of Congress Control Number: 2007938368

Published by

TEACH Services, Inc.
www.TEACHServices.com

CONTENTS

PREFACE

I received my training in counseling psychology over 18 years ago. When I started my work as a psychologist, I was excited because I sincerely believed that the concepts I had learned could be used to help many people, especially my Christian brothers and sisters. I began my career in academia teaching at the college level for about six years. After leaving this arena, I worked as a therapist in private practice and have been in that setting for the past 12 to 13 years.

One day, about two years ago, I happened to come across a sermon by a pastor who delineated several spiritual dangers inherent in the field of psychology.* Initially, I was not happy about what I read in this sermon because the writer attacked most, if not all, that I had been taught as a psychologist. But as the Holy Spirit worked on my heart and led me to study this issue further, I finally had to admit that many concepts in secular psychology are in direct conflict with the Word of God.

What an eye-opening experience this was for me!

Since that time, the Lord has given me several opportunities to share with my Christian brethren what I have learned. Many of those who felt they were blessed by this information have been encouraging me to put all this material into a book. Because I felt this was the leading of the Holy Spirit, I decided to listen. The book in your hand is the final result!

I must say that the enemy is crafty and has weaved a tight "web" of secular psychology around the Christian church. This is evident to me as I observe more and more Christians turning to psychologists and other types of therapists for help with personal issues, marital and family problems, and workplace and social struggles.

*NOTE: As I use the word psychology throughout this book, I am specifically referring to clinical/counseling psychology. I do realize that there are other disciplines of psychology that have been beneficial in helping us understand the functioning of the brain and human behavior, similar to the way the study of anatomy and physiology helps us understand the body.

In addition, I have become aware of how the philosophies of secular psychology are increasingly guiding the programs and even the mission of the Christian church. Because this "web" of deception is so tightly woven around the minds of Christians, I realize that only through prayer and the sincere study of God's Word can the enemy's delusions in this area be "unmasked." I believe that all things are possible through God!

Dear reader, as you go through this book, it is my prayer that you will allow your mind to be open to the information that will be shared. Even more important, it is my strong admonition that you closely compare what I have written with the Word of God and reject anything that is not in accordance with it.

It is my hope that we, as individuals, will learn that we can turn to God for help with *every* problem that comes our way. It is also my desire that, on a corporate level, we will realize that God's Word contains all that we need to have a flourishing, vibrant church.

Again I say, all things are possible through God!

FOREWORD

For years the Christian and non-Christian alike have wrestled with various problems of living, and often concluded that these problems could not be managed without professional help. That has usually meant someone with training in counseling and working as a psychologist or a psychiatrist.

Along with time spent in the office of the professional counselor usually comes a healthy dose of thinking from the secular world through its most prominent spokespersons, such authorities as Freud, Rogers, Maslow, and many others. Their theories become the guide to resolving the person's needs.

Is it possible that an undue emphasis on concepts not supported by God's word could actually be dangerous to our spiritual growth? Is it possible that the enemy of our souls has actually woven a web of secular psychology around the church that blocks out the need to turn to God for help? What if this ideology, a cunning blend of truth and lies, has infiltrated every aspect of our Christian lives—our attitudes and behavior, our programs and philosophies, even the way we worship?

This book by an experienced psychologist, who is also a Christian, breaks new ground in the way it views the field of secular psychology. It is an absolutely unique perspective I have not read before. It is biblical, well written, extensively documented, and clearly explained.

After Seminary, I decided to pursue a degree in psychology. I began doing part-time class work while pastoring. Early on, the chair of the psychology department, a Baptist professor, told me at the end of his class that he had all of Ellen White's books, and that our church was wonderfully blessed with heavenly insights. He said that if people would simply follow scriptural principles and the additional insights of Ellen White, all but those with serious mental illness would find the answers to their problems, without counseling. He had some of the same concerns as those expressed by Dr. Parks. For solving member problems, he wanted pastors to focus more on the teachings of scripture than on the concepts of modern psychology.

While this book is certain to be controversial, I would hope it leads to meaningful thought and discussion in a most important area of life. If one person can be freed from an unhealthy dependence on the thinking of men, and turned to the source of all truth, it will have been worth the effort to bring it to print.

The pages to come offer you an informative and exciting journey.

Thomas Mostert, President
Pacific Union Conference

FOREWORD

It has been very satisfying to pick up this book, catch the author's scholarly insights, definitions and conclusions which are anchored in her absolute trust in God and His unalterable WORD.

For many, the element of "faith" is too nebulous and subjective, and lacking this, they yearn for scientific solutions and pronouncements which they consider to be authentic and dependable. In this they exercise "faith", also. The difference is that instead of faith in God, they place their trust in credentialed men and their theories which inevitably counter each other in serious contradiction. This causes the resulting doubts and fears to proliferate and causes them to choose which authority they will accept. Thus the problem—instead of being solved is seriously exacerbated.

The author of this volume is not a prisoner of her faith—she has been set free by it. Her anchor is the Word of God—that Word often maligned and derided. Her trust shines through her writing with confidence and assurance. Her God cannot lie (Titus 1:2) and over the centuries His Word has stood the test of assaults and bitter opposition. Dr. Parks doesn't denounce psychology—only that area of it that contradicts the known Word of God. The world's "best seller" is still the Holy Bible.

Dr. Parks hopes that her readers will discover how precious, how beautiful, how reasonable, how unerring how dependable that Word is. Only those aspects of psychology which will rob us of TRUTH are identified. She remains committed to her field and to her clients and will bring the same devotion to her work which you will discover in this book. Would you like to know what TRUTH is? Then, read John 17:17. And enjoy this volume.

Dr. Charles D. Brooks, Speaker Emeritus
BREATH of LIFE Television Ministry

CHAPTER 1

A CLEVER STRATEGY: A LITTLE TRUTH, A LOT OF ERROR

"And the serpent said unto the woman, 'Ye shall not surely die; for God doth know that in the day ye eat thereof, then your eyes shall be opened, and ye shall be as gods, knowing good and evil" (Gen. 3:4, 5)

From the beginning of time, starting with our first parents, Satan has used deception to lead God's people away from belief in His Word. But how do you confuse people who have had access to a great deal of truth? How do you confuse a mind such as Eve's, straight from the hand of God?

Satan's clever solution: pretend to present truth, but mix a small amount of error with it. This has been one of his most masterful strategies for deceiving otherwise bright people.

In the verse above, we see that the truth in Satan's statement to Eve is that when she (and Adam) ate the fruit their eyes were opened—that is, opened to a knowledge of evil that heretofore they had not known. However, the error in what he told Eve was that they would not die. At the moment, when they partook of the fruit Adam and Eve did not experience immediate death. But true to God's Word, as a result of their sin, death eventually came not only to them but also to the whole world. Satan seems to have sensed that if he came to Eve with straight error she would not have easily fallen for his temptation. So he had to mix it with truth in order to achieve his goal. It is stated that:

> "Error cannot stand alone, and would soon become extinct
> if it did not fasten itself like a parasite upon the tree of truth.
> Error draws its life from the truth of God."[1]

Since the Fall, Satan has time again served this "deadly potion" of truth mixed with error to deceive God's people. Unfortunately, a review of the Bible and human history reveals that he has been quite successful!

1

How, then, does this relate to psychology and the church? It is my belief that secular psychology has been readily and almost unreservedly accepted by many Christians because it is composed of truth mixed with error. Many of the theories and concepts of psychology have grains of truth embedded within. It is this that makes them so very dangerous.

I am an example of someone who fell for this trap. But when I was led to the truth through God's Word, I realized that I had been deceived by the enemy and had to admit that "the wisdom of this world is foolishness with God" (1 Cor. 3:19). I also realized that there is "no new thing under the sun." The enemy used his strategy, deception, successfully in the past, and he would use it again and again, until the end of time.

CHAPTER 2

WHERE DID PSYCHOLOGY COME FROM?

Psychology traces its roots to philosophy. In general, the field of philosophy is one that seeks to understand concepts such as knowledge, morality, existence, beauty, and truth.[1] Interestingly, these are the same basic issues that are addressed by religion.

Before psychology became a discipline, various philosophers laid its foundation. Two of the earliest philosophers, Aristotle and Socrates, encouraged humans to "know" themselves and to "know" behavior.

Another philosopher who had a significant impact on psychology was Rene Descartes. Also a mathematician and physiologist, Descartes is considered the first great psychologist of the modern age, even before modern psychology was founded.[2] Descartes glorified reason in that he believed that only through reason can we know truth.[3] It was Descartes who coined the phrase, "I think therefore I am."

Many other philosophers were instrumental in establishing a foundation for the discipline of psychology. For purposes of this book, however, we will fast-forward to the year 1590, when Rudolph Glocenius, a German philosopher, was the first to use the word "psychology." Even though he introduced what was then considered a new concept, psychology continued to be considered a branch of philosophy for almost three hundred more years.

The separation of psychology from philosophy began when Wilhelm Wundt developed the first scientific psychology laboratory in Germany. In this laboratory he ran various experiments, so to speak, in which he attempted to study the mind and behavior.

A few years later, William James, one of the first American psychologists, wrote a classic textbook, *Principles of Psychology*, which laid the foundation for modern psychology. It should be noted that James's approach to psychology was partly influenced by Charles Darwin's theory of evolution, which was introduced in 1859.

Both Wilhelm Wundt and William James are credited with "freeing" psychology from its philosophical roots, thereby establishing the field of modern psychology.

Description of Modern Psychology

Modern psychology is the scientific study of behavior and mental processes, which can be traced back to the philosophical concepts introduced by Aristotle, Socrates, and Descartes. Behavior is considered to be everything we do that can be directly observed. Mental processes "describe the thoughts, feelings, and motives that each of us experience privately but that cannot be observed directly."[4]

Psychologists purport that the study of behaviors, thoughts, feelings, and motives can help us better understand human functioning and more effectively address emotional, mental, and social problems. The assumption is that the more we know about ourselves as human beings, the better people we can be.

Clinical/Counseling Psychology

There are numerous disciplines within the field of psychology including social psychology, experimental psychology, neuropsychology, and counseling/clinical psychology. The latter discipline, counseling/clinical psychology,* the focus of this book, seeks to apply psychological principles to the treatment of mental and emotional disorders and to address problems of everyday living, such as marital and family concerns, parenting issues, social relationships and related areas. This branch of psychology comprises most of what the average layperson thinks about when he or she uses the word "psychology." As a result, it is this psychological discipline that has had the greatest influence on various sectors of our society, including the Christian church.

*Within the field of psychology, these two areas, counseling and clinical psychology, are technically considered to be separate. In reality, however, the disciplines are similar, and psychologists trained in either tend to do similar work.

CHAPTER 3

WHY WE ARE AS WE ARE:
POPULAR PSYCHOLOGY THEORIES

Within the fields of clinical/counseling psychology, there are differences of opinion about human nature and human functioning. This has led to the development of a number of perspectives (also known as theories) about why we are the way we are and how we can change.

The three theories that have had the most influence in our culture are the psychoanalytic, behaviorist, and humanistic perspectives. The two that have had the greatest influence on Christianity are the psychoanalytic and the humanistic perspectives.

Psychoanalytic Theory

Psychoanalytic theory was introduced by Sigmund Freud, a medical doctor who specialized in the field of neurology but later became interested in psychology. Freud believed that human beings do not have free will and that their actions, thoughts, feelings, and words are motivated by material in the mind of which they are unaware (the unconscious).

One of the major sources of unconscious material is childhood experience. Freud purported that problems in later life are due to events in our childhood, especially as related to our experiences with our parents. In order to resolve these problems, we *must* be able to remember and talk about our childhood experiences and learn how they affect our current lives.

Freud's theory laid the foundation for what would become known as "talk therapy," which mental health professionals generally refer to as "psychotherapy." With this type of therapy, people are encouraged to have conversations, so to speak, with a counselor or therapist, who reportedly helps them understand and resolve their problems. In many cases, the focus of this understanding is to learn how past experiences affect current functioning.

This concept is one that has become so popular that it is no longer necessary for people to attend therapy to apply it (or learn about it). There are workshops, books, television shows and movies that reportedly help people learn more about themselves by focusing on childhood experiences.

Fromm and Unconditional Love

A number of individuals followed Freud initially, but later disagreed with some of his ideas and developed their own theories. One such person was Erich Fromm. Fromm believed that human beings are motivated by social and cultural influences and not merely by unconscious forces. For example, he viewed love as having a significant impact on human behavior. This was in contrast to Freud, who did not believe love had much impact on human actions.

In 1956, Fromm wrote a book entitled *The Art of Loving*, in which he defined love as supreme and unconditional. It is from this definition that the phrase "unconditional love" was derived. Fromm also taught that one must love self, accept self, and esteem self in order to reach one's highest potential.[1] This teaching is also espoused by humanistic psychologists, and will be discussed later in this chapter.

Freud and Religion

Freud, a Jew by birth, was an atheist. He categorized religion as something that is based on wishful thinking, which he referred to as an "illusion." Freud believed that religion is comparable to "childhood neurosis"—basically, a child's fear and need for help. Freud also purported that human beings turn to religion because of a need for guidance from a powerful father and to gain relief from suffering.

Humanistic Theory

Humanistic psychology focuses on the individual choices and personal freedoms of human beings. The belief is that human nature is basically "good" and that we are born with the tendency to fulfill our potential in life. Two of the most prominent psychologists who laid the foundation for humanistic theory are Carl Rogers and Abraham Maslow.

Carl Rogers and "Self"

Carl Rogers is the founder of what is known as "self psychology." As the name suggests, this theory views the self as a central aspect of human functioning. Rogers and other humanistic psychologists contend that the self is developed through one's interactions with others. The way in which we view our abilities, behavior, and personality is known as our "self-concept."

According to Rogers, our self-concepts are based on how we are treated by others. For example, he maintained that we develop a poor self-concept when others, such as parents, siblings, or teachers, do not accept us for who we are, and give us love and praise only when we conform to their standards, which he calls "conditions of worth." Rogers believed that a person who has a poor self-concept is likely to think, feel, and act negatively. [2]

On the other hand, when individuals receive what Rogers calls "unconditional positive regard," which means that they are accepted and valued regardless of their behavior, then they are more likely to have a healthy self-concept.

Rogers' theory has had a significant impact on the discipline of psychology. For example, in the area of counseling and therapy, counselors are taught that they should show an unconditional attitude toward their clients. In other words, they should accept their clients as they are and not allow their own values to influence the way in which they view them. The belief is that if clients are treated in this way, they are more likely to overcome their emotional problems. This assumption also goes beyond the counseling office. The idea that we should accept people as they are and make no judgments about their behaviors is prevalent in contemporary society; an example of this is the "politically-correct" movement.

Rogers and Religion

Rogers grew up in a religious home. He made a decision to enter the ministry when he was a young person. However, it did not take long before he began to doubt the strict religious worldview of his parents. He attended a liberal seminary and while he was there he began to develop his own worldview. Rogers then chose a different career, one that would not require him to believe in specific religious doctrines. He preferred a field that would allow him more freedom of thought, so he decided to become a psychologist.

Abraham Maslow and Needs

The second psychologist who had a significant influence on the development of humanistic psychology is Abraham Maslow. Maslow believed that human beings are motivated by what he called a "hierarchy of needs." According to Maslow, the most basic needs that we have are physical needs for food, water, shelter, and safety. After these needs are met, then "higher" needs emerge, such as the needs for love, for a sense of belonging, and for esteem.

The highest need on Maslow's hierarchy is self-actualization, which refers to the need we have to fulfill our potential as human beings. This is a state of being, according to Maslow, which is reached by very few people. He identified and studied the lives of several individuals, including Thomas Jefferson, Abraham Lincoln, Albert Einstein, and Frederick Douglas, who he believe achieved this level of functioning. He referred to these persons as "self-actualizers."

Maslow's ideas have been incorporated into various sectors of our society. In the education arena, administrators and teachers are encouraged to consider the needs of students in developing methods to help them achieve in school. For example, it is recognized that if students are hungry (a lower need), they will not learn well (a higher need). The advent of free breakfasts and lunch programs was a direct result of such considerations.[3]

Also, teachers are encouraged to help students feel good about themselves (self-esteem needs) because it is believed that this will help them perform better academically (self-actualization).

In the business sector, Maslow's concepts are utilized to motivate employees. For example, efforts are made by some organizations to help employees feel a sense of belonging and acceptance, or to encourage them to feel good about themselves as a means of helping them to be more productive at work.

Maslow and Religion

Maslow believed that traditional religion was inadequate to help human beings. He disagreed with several of its teachings, such as the belief that negative emotions and behaviors result from sin. For Maslow, it was the denial or suppression of needs or desires that led to problem behaviors and emotions. Maslow's goal was to displace traditional religion with a "science of man."[4] It should be mentioned that much of his thinking was inspired by Zen Buddhism and Taoism, both Eastern religions.

CHAPTER 4

CHRISTIANITY EMBRACES SECULAR PSYCHOLOGY

Abraham Maslow made the following statement about psychology:

> "Indeed, I sometimes think that the world will either be saved by psychologists—in the very broadest sense—or else it will not be saved at all."[1]

Most psychologists and other mental health experts probably hold this view, consciously or unconsciously. But is this a view also held by Christians?

Sad to say, the answer is yes. This is evident when we observe more and more of God's people turning to psychology almost as a type of savior to help them with their difficulties, both in their personal lives and in the church.

How and when did Christians begin to embrace secular psychology in this way? The following quotation gives some insight:

> "The encroachment of the psychology way into Christianity has been a subtle, gradual movement which began in seminaries and pastoral counseling classes. Pastors were concerned about their parishioners seeking help outside the fold and so they availed themselves of the wisdom of men in order to minister to souls."[2]

Another author indicates that many pastors "accepted the lie that they could only deal with spiritual matters and that only those who were psychologically trained were equipped to deal with psychological matters."[3]

So here we see the beginning of psychology being viewed as a viable source of help for Christians. As more began to turn to psychology for their personal difficulties, this opened the door for the entrance of secular psychological concepts into the church on a corporate level.

Some may be asking, what is wrong with this? On the surface, the entrance of secular psychology into the Christian church might appear innocent, even helpful. But upon closer inspection, the discerning eye will see that it is fraught with spiritual dangers, which we explore further in the next few chapters.

CHAPTER 5

CHRISTIANS NEED TO UNDERSTAND CHILD-HOOD, RIGHT?

The belief that we should focus on childhood experiences to better understand ourselves has become very popular in Christian circles. Over the past thirty years or so, Christians have become increasingly interested in talking about their childhood and learning about how it has affected them. Many have turned to psychologists and other mental health professionals to gain more of an understanding in this area.

In addition, there are a plethora of programs, workshops, and seminars on this topic that have been attended by thousands of Christians. Some of the buzzwords associated with these programs include "healing the inner child," "healing wounds," or "binding wounds."

Many Christians now believe that one must understand and work through past childhood experiences to achieve emotional healing and even spiritual growth. For example, one well-known TV minister states that if we don't deal with the "little boy or girl inside" we cannot know the 'God of the Bible'"[1]

This thinking has also been embraced by more than just a few Seventh-day Adventists. Over the years, the number of Seventh-day Adventists seeking therapy has been increasing. In addition, more and more churches are sponsoring programs that reportedly help members understand how their childhood has affected them.

For years, I myself promoted this idea in the workshops and seminars that I presented in churches. I believed and taught that in order for Christians to be "whole" they must understand, through the theories of secular psychology, the impact of their childhood on their current functioning. But is this true?

What is the Truth about Childhood Experiences?

To put it simply, the idea that we must understand childhood to resolve our problems is false. I have come to regard this concept as erroneous, and have confirmed it as such in my work with clients. For example, as a therapist, I have had cases in which people have come to me "armed" with knowledge about the impact of their childhood on their current lives. Most of these individuals gained this information from previous therapists, television programs, workshops, or self-help books.

However, in spite of all the insight they gained about their childhood, many of them continued to have problems in various areas of their lives. They appeared to be "stuck" and were not making any progress emotionally, and for those who were Christians, spiritually. In some cases, it appeared that the more these individuals thought they knew about themselves, the more difficulties they seemed to have.

Focusing on Childhood Keeps Us In Bondage!

Why isn't it helpful to focus on our past to help us with our emotional difficulties, especially as Christians? For one, focusing on the past keeps us in bondage to the past. This is why we are told by Paul that we should be *"forgetting those things which are behind,* and reaching forth unto those things which are before, (to) press toward the mark for the prize of the high calling of God in Christ Jesus" (Phil. 3:13, 14).

How can we fulfill this spiritual goal if we spend time analyzing and gaining supposed insight into what our parents and others have done to hurt us when we were children?

In addition, God tells us that "if any man be in Christ, he is a new creature: old things are passed away; behold, all things are become new" (2 Cor. 5:17). If we are truly born again, we must realize that whatever we experienced when we were children is now "passed away."

This undue focus on childhood can prevent us from developing our new lives in Christ— just what Satan desires. This is why we are admonished to "cast out of the mind the dangerous, obtrusive theories which, if entertained, will hold the mind in bondage so that the man shall not become a new creature in Christ."[2] Could such "theories" include those from the secular psychology world? I believe the answer is yes!

It Also Masks The Real Cause of Our Problems!

Another concern with this emphasis on childhood is that it blinds us to the real nature of our problems as human beings— *SIN*. It is true that our parents, and others in our families, often make serious mistakes that may have an impact on us. However, we cannot excuse ourselves because of their shortcomings. God holds us individually responsible for the decisions and choices we make. He tells us that "all have sinned, and come short of the glory of God" (Rom. 3:23) and that "we shall all stand before the judgment seat of Christ" (Rom. 14:10). It is only when we recognize that we are personally responsible for many of our problems that we can truly begin to resolve them.

In order to obtain true healing, oftentimes we must identify and acknowledge our sin and then turn to the Savior for the power to overcome. This is something we can never accomplish with secular psychology.*

Can We Truly Know Ourselves?

This belief about understanding childhood seems to be based on the assumption that the more we know ourselves, the better we can control our lives—an idea mentioned earlier as the essence of modern psychology. But, the question is, can we really *know* ourselves? The Bible tells us,"the heart is deceitful above all things, and desperately wicked: who can know it?" (Jer. 17:9).

No matter how many years one spends in a therapist's office, reading self-help books, or attending workshops that focus on childhood, the truth is that only the Holy Spirit can reveal who we are and how we came to be that way.

The second danger, or error, in this quest to "know" ourselves is that it is very similar to the ideology Satan used in the Garden of Eden. He said, "that in the day ye eat thereof, then your eyes

---

* I do not believe that all psychological problems are caused by individual sin, *per se*. Some disorders are attributed to obvious physical problems, such as diseases or dysfunctions of the brain or body or both, or even poor lifestyle choices, which I will briefly discuss later in this book. Such problems or disorders must be treated with the help of knowledgeable health professionals.

shall be opened, and ye shall be as gods, *knowing* good and evil" (Gen. 3:5). Implicit in his statement was that increased knowledge brings increased power. I believe that this is what makes the idea of psychological insight into childhood so attractive. Such knowledge appears to place us on a higher plane, so to speak—one that almost makes us think we are gods. But this idea is a deceptive trap of the enemy to make us more self-reliant and less dependent on God. Sooner or later, we will discover that self-knowledge is powerless to help us truly resolve our problems.

Memories of Childhood Can be False

Before ending this section, I would like to discuss briefly, from a secular perspective, a significant concern that must be considered if we look to the past to help us with our present lives: the memories of our childhood can be distorted or even false.

Elizabeth Loftus, a psychologist who has done significant work in memory research, states the following:

> "With the passage of time, with proper motivation, with the introduction of special kinds of interfering facts, the memory traces seem sometimes to change or become transformed. These distortions can be quite frightening, for they can cause us to have memories of things that never happened."[3]

The fact that our memories can be inaccurate presents a major problem if we are relying on our recollection of childhood experiences to resolve our difficulties. For example, there have been cases of individuals who regained alleged "memories" of childhood events from sources such as self-help books, talk shows, or even a therapist, and it was later determined that such memories were inaccurate or completely false.

What makes this issue even more problematic is that false memories can lead to even more difficulties, such as a breakdown of family relationships. For example, I've heard of therapy cases in which individuals were led to believe that, as children, they were sexually abused by a particular parent. These persons then made the decision (or were encouraged by their therapists) to distance themselves from this parent and/or other family members. As a result, a host of additional problems developed. Thus, the supposed insight gained about the impact of their childhood on their current lives ended up being more hurtful than helpful.

In summary, the "truth" of Freud's theory is that focusing on the past cannot help us with our present difficulties. When we are faced with problems, we must focus on the present and ask God to reveal to us what we need to change and give us the power to do so. In some cases, there may not be much we can change, but we can seek God's strength to cope with whatever He allows to come our way.

CHAPTER 6

GOD WANTS ME TO FEEL GOOD ABOUT MYSELF, DOESN'T HE?

The humanistic approach is that branch of clinical/counseling psychology that has probably had the greatest impact on Christians and the church. One of the main reasons for this is that many of the concepts of humanistic psychology resemble the principles of Christianity, such as the idea that we should love and care for others and that we should not judge others.[1]

This truth-error mixture has been deadly for Christians in that it has led many, knowingly or unknowingly, to turn more to humanistic psychology than to God for help with their problems.

The Christian and Self-Esteem

One of the most widespread humanistic concepts to be accepted in Christian circles is that of self-esteem. As touted by psychologists Carl Rogers and Abraham Maslow, self-esteem is considered important for one to be happy and mentally healthy. Some Christians even believe that self-love or self-esteem is necessary for spiritual growth. Many use the Scriptural injunction to "love thy neighbor as thyself" as proof for their belief that God encourages us to develop a healthy self-esteem.

This concept has become ingrained in the psyche of many Christians. As a psychologist, I have had quite a few of these individuals coming to my office and attributing their problems to low self-esteem. They assume that if they can obtain help to raise their self-esteem, their difficulties will be resolved.

Self-Esteem Comes to Church

This thinking about self-esteem is also reflected in various facets of the church. For example, over the years I have observed an increasing number of Christian authors, even within the Seventh-day Adventist Church, promote the idea that self-esteem is important for God's professed people. Consider the following quotation from a Sabbath School quarterly:

> "....The first thing Jesus does is to tell Simon Peter the work He is going to have him do. Perhaps Jesus, *knowing Peter's lack of self-esteem*, immediately told him of his important task in order to help Peter understand that although he was a sinner, Christ not only accepted him, but was going to trust him with important work."[2]

The reference is to Christ's initial meeting with Peter after His resurrection. The author seems to imply that there was a relationship between Peter's self-esteem and his denial of Christ—that either Peter denied Christ because he had a low self-esteem or that his self-esteem was affected by denial of Christ. Thus, Christ had to build up Peter's esteem by letting him know that he accepted and trusted him to do work for the church. Sounds plausible but, again, is it true?

Corporate Worship: The Place to Promote Self-Esteem?

Another area in the church where this self-esteem focus has had a significant impact is in corporate worship. The thinking seems to be that the church should put forth efforts to ensure that members feel good about (or esteem) themselves.

This philosophy has been a major impetus for the growth of what is known as the Contemporary Christian Music Movement (CCM), which seems to be a close cousin to the Celebration worship movement that was popular in some Seventh-day Adventist churches a few years ago.

Briefly, the CCM movement incorporates elements of worship that is reflective of contemporary society, such as modern music styles, dress, language and other aspects of our current culture. One of the underlying assumptions of CCM worship is that God wants to "affirm us through worship, to make us *feel good about ourselves*."[3] A former CCM worship leader states it in this way:

"In my own experience, I noticed that we Contemporaries (proponents of the CCM movement) preferred to raise our faces and hands up to God and called that worship... I thought back to when I first changed my... worship style from bowing my head to looking up.... I remember the good feeling it gave me that I was for the first time a participant in worship *with* God, not some lowly worm, who had to prostrate myself. *I felt better about myself.*"[4]

This push toward helping church members feel good about self is also reflected in other aspects of the worship service (which may have little to do with the CCM movement). For example, there have been changes made in songs, such as hymns, that seem to reflect this self-esteem focus. An illustration of this is the hymn *At The Cross*. In the former Seventh-day Adventist hymnal, the words of this song were as follows:

> *Alas and did my Savior bleed,*
> *and did my Sovereign die?*
> *Would He devote that sacred head*
> *for <u>such a worm as I</u>?*

In the current Seventh-day Adventist hymnal the words now read,

> *Alas and did my Savior bleed,*
> *and did my Sovereign die?*
> *Would He devote that sacred head*
> *for <u>someone such as I</u>?*

This change was originally carried out by a non-S.D.A denomination and was subsequently followed by others, including the Seventh-day Adventist church. From a purely human perspective, wouldn't you admit that it feels better to be referred to as "someone" rather than as a "worm?" It is this type of rationale that has propelled this and other such changes in the Christian church. But as we shall later see, such ideas have come with a price that has high spiritual costs, on both an individual and a corporate level.

Applaud and Recognition At Church

There are many other examples of efforts being made within the church to ensure that members feel good about self (or have a positive self-esteem). For example, if you attend many churches today, it is not uncommon to read or hear about people being recognized for their birthdays, anniversaries, and other milestones. Also, it has become quite popular for members to be awarded with plaques or other tokens of commendation for their work either inside or outside of the church—and the list can go on and on.

Suffice it to say that any practice that relies solely on human effort to applaud, recognize, or uplift others reflects the philosophy that we should feel good about self. I must add that those who have incorporated these changes are likely sincere in their efforts and view these practices as having a positive impact. However, as I heard one pastor put it, these same individuals do not realize that they are "picking the fruit, without identifying the root" (humanistic psychology) of these practices.[5]

What Is the Truth about Self-Esteem?

Esteem Self or Deny Self?

Does this humanistic focus on self-esteem fit with what we are told about "self" in God's Word? Consider the following scriptural passages:

> "If any man will come after me, let him *deny* him*self*, and take up his cross, and follow me" (Matt. 16:24*)*.

> "Let nothing be done through strife or vainglory; but in lowliness of mind let each *esteem other better than themselves*" (Phil. 2:3)

What do these two verses teach us about how Christians should respond to "self"? In the first, Jesus tells us that to follow Him we must *deny* self. Is it possible to increase our esteem of self while at the same time denying self? To deny self is to "renounce (self)…henceforth to live for Christ rather than for one's (self)."[6] When we examine the life of Christ, who is our example, it is apparent that He spent more time denying self than seeking to enhance self (or looking for others to do the same).

In the second verse, Paul admonishes us to esteem others *better* than ourselves. Can we seek to increase our self-esteem while also esteeming others better than ourselves? In spite what secular psychology tells us, the answer is no.

It should be clear, then, that the view of self espoused by humanistic psychology contradicts the Word of God. The following quotations expound on the Biblical view of self-esteem:

> "We must realize that we are in Christ's school, *not to learn how we may esteem ourselves*....but how we may cherish the meekness of Christ."[7]

> "If you will sincerely humble your hearts before Him (God), *empty your souls of self-esteem* and put away the natural defects of your character. He will bestow on you His Holy Spirit."[8]

Given what God tells us in His Word and other inspired writings, this push for self-esteem is in direct conflict with what He asks of us as His professed people. My fear is that individually and corporately, the enemy of our souls is deceiving Christians into placing more effort on esteeming self than on heeding God's Word and emulating Christ's example. Without giving him too much credit, I must say that this is a crafty plan and he has, unfortunately, been quite successful with it.

Self-Worth, Self-Respect and the Christian

Does this caution about self-esteem mean that Christians should view themselves negatively and have a low opinion of self? No, not at all! The gospel is the good news that Christ left heaven to pay the penalty for our sins and to give us power to overcome sin. When we contemplate Christ's sacrifice and all that has been expended on our behalf, we see the high price that was paid for our redemption. It is only as we gain a spiritual understanding of this reality that we can have a proper understanding of self—we are worth something (*self-worth, not self-esteem*) because of what God has done for us. As human beings we are limited in what we can do to develop a proper self-image. True self-worth can come only by understanding God's love for us as exhibited through the life and death (and mediation) of His Son. As stated:

"It is through the cross alone that we can estimate the worth of the human soul. Such is the value of men for whom Christ died....The worth of man is known only by going to Calvary."[9]

This is why Paul says in Galatians 6:14, "But God forbid that I should glory, save in the cross of our Lord Jesus Christ..."

There is another aspect of our self-worth that is largely ignored by the humanistic concept of self-esteem. This is described in the following quotation:

"It is not pleasing to God that you should demerit yourself. You should cultivate a *self-respect by living so that you will be approved by your own conscience, and before men and angels*...While we should not think of ourselves more highly than we ought, the Word of God does not condemn a proper self-respect. As sons and daughters of God, we should have a conscious dignity of character, in which pride and self-importance have no part."[10]

According to the servant of the Lord, our view of self is also influenced by the lives that we live. Specifically, if we are engaging in thoughts, attitudes, behaviors, and feelings that God can approve of, then we will develop a self-view, a self-respect, that is in accordance with His will. On the other hand, if we are persistently living in a manner that violates our conscience and God's commands, this will lead to a lack of respect for self and, in turn, a lowered sense of self-worth.

More Evidence Against Self-Esteem: Secular Perspectives

Interestingly, some in the field of psychology do understand that the traditional humanistic view of self-esteem is not as beneficial as many believe. Consider the findings of the following study:

"....College students who (base) their self-worth on *external* sources—including appearance, approval from others, and even academic performance—reported (high) stress, anger, academic problems, relationship conflicts, and had high levels of drug and alcohol use and symptoms of eating disorders....Students who based their self-esteem on *internal* sources—such as *being a virtuous person or adhering to moral standards*—were found to have higher grades and were less likely to use alcohol and drugs or to develop eating disorders..."[11]

The authors of this study then conclude:

> "We really think that if people could adopt goals *not fo-cused on their own self-esteem* but on *something larger than their self*—then they would be *less susceptible to some of the negative effects of pursuing self-esteem.*"[12]

Interestingly, the results of this study are clearly congruent with the previous quotation in which we are told that to obtain a proper view of self we should live to be approved by (our) *"own conscience and before men and angels."*

Further evidence from the secular world reveals that this self-esteem focus has not yielded the promising results touted by proponents of humanistic psychology. In the late 1980s a task force at the University of California looked at research on self-esteem as related to various problems, such as alcohol and drug abuse, crime, violence and recidivism, welfare dependency, children failing in school, teenage pregnancy, and abuse of children and spouses. Their review of the research basically revealed no causal relationship between low self-esteem and these problematic behaviors.[13]

In other words, low self-esteem was not found to cause, per se, any of the above-stated problems, thus contradicting popular thinking that individuals with these issues lack self-esteem. On the other hand, there is research that suggests that those with high self-esteem display various problematic behaviors including classroom violence, certain types of crime, hostility toward others, and aggressive behavior.[14]

So here we have evidence from the secular world that supports the principles stated in God's Word thousands of years earlier. In spite of this, there are those in society and in the Christian church who continue to push the false notions about self-esteem. Why is this so? Could it be that the enemy of souls wants to keep as many as he can under his control by blinding us to the truth? It seems that this may be the case. Remember, he is the "father of lies."

CHAPTER 7

GOD AND OTHERS MUST LOVE ME UNCONDITIONALLY

It is popular among many Christians today to describe God's love as "unconditional" and to encourage the idea that we should display this same type of love toward each other. This thinking comes from another humanistic concept that has been widely accepted in Christian circles, that of unconditional love and acceptance (introduced by Erich Fromm and Carl Rogers).

There is some truth to this thinking. It is true, for example, that we should not set "conditions" that people must reach in order for us to love and accept them. Most of us want to know that we are loved for who we are and not because of what we do. And it is also true that God does not require us to fulfill any "conditions" before He will love us. In fact, Paul tells us in Romans 5:8, "God commendeth His love toward us, in that, while we were yet sinners, Christ died for us." Thus, there is nothing we can do, per se, to obtain God's love.

However, the issue does not end here, as we will see later in this chapter. There is more that we need to understand about this concept of unconditional love.

God Accepts Me—You Should Too!

The promotion of this unconditional love/acceptance philosophy has encouraged many Christians to believe that they can do almost whatever they want in their lives. The thought is that if God accepts us as we are, we can eat as we please, entertain as we please, dress as we please, work as we please, and even worship as we please. And we dare not make any comments to other Christians about their lifestyle—how they eat, dress, or worship—because this would be viewed as not loving or accepting them unconditionally. As stated by one author:

> "Acceptance doctrine (the idea that we should accept one another unconditionally) is so pervasive in some fellowships that

Christians are no longer allowed to question another Christian's behavior or personal preferences. If you confront another in love, you will be accused of judging them. If you dare quote chapter and verse from the Bible, you will be called a Pharisee. If a church has any practices that step on the toes of anyone's personal preferences, then it is considered to be a legalistic church."[1]

This concept of unconditional love and acceptance has spawned the "come as you are" philosophy that is touted by many churches. The idea is that we should not be urged to change any aspects of our lifestyle because God accepts and love us as we are.

Acceptance Doctrine and the Church

How is this idea about unconditional love/acceptance manifested in our churches? The examples are numerous. For one, there is a growing trend, especially in the Seventh-day Adventist church, for members to be instructed not to say anything to newly baptized members, young people, or others about their dress, worship, adornment, etc. The fear is that if we focus too much on such issues, we will "run" these members out of the church. We are encouraged, instead, to accept and love them unconditionally, because it is believed they will eventually make the needed changes in their lifestyles. And if they don't change, we are reminded that God is the "ultimate judge."

Another example of the impact of this unconditional love/acceptance philosophy is in the area of church attire. In general, it is now acceptable to dress casually, or "dress down," for church. For example, in many churches today it is common to see men with no ties or suits, women wearing pants or pant suits, and young people wearing casual clothes.

Many congregations are now using this "come as you are" philosophy as a strategy to draw people to their churches. I cannot tell you the numerous postcards and flyers I have received in the mail from churches in the area that encourage people to visit their places of worship in "casual" or "comfortable" attire.

Yet another area that has been influenced by this "acceptance" concept is that of corporate worship. As stated by one author, "If God accepts me as I am, then surely He accepts my personal preferences in worship . . . .God knows I'm not perfect and He still loves me, so how can anyone else hold me accountable for my actions?"[2] As a result, there can be no talk about "proper worship" because God accepts whatever we choose to bring to Him. It is believed that this "acceptance doctrine" has encouraged the embracing of the Contemporary Christian Music Movement by many Christians.[3]

What Is the Truth about Unconditional Love?

Is this philosophy of unconditional love and acceptance from God and others congruent with God's Word? It is clear (as stated earlier in this section) that God does not expect us to fulfill any conditions before He bestows His love upon us. Remember, the subtle deception of these humanistic concepts for Christians is that they are mixed with some truth and *a lot* of error. Even though God may initially bestow His love without asking anything from us, does it stop there? Consider the words of Jesus:

> "He that hath my commandments, and keepeth them, he it is that loveth me: and he that loveth me *shall be loved of my father*, and I will love him, and will manifest myself to him." (John 14:21)

In other words, we show our love to God by following His commandments. Also interesting in this verse is the thought that the exhibition of our love to Him (by keeping His commandments) is somehow connected to the love that He displays toward us.

Again, not that His love is contingent upon our obeying Him, *but* Jesus tells us there is some relationship between the two. The danger in using the humanistic concept of "unconditionality" to describe God's love is that it disconnects us from His requirements, such as the keeping of His commandments.

God's Love Cannot Ignore Sin

Another problem can occur when we spend too much time focusing on the nature of God's love as unconditional. Consider the following:

> "This goody-goody religion that makes light of sin and that is forever dwelling upon the love of God to the sinner, encour-

ages the sinner to believe that God will save him while he continues in sin and knows it to be sin." [4]

This is exactly what the enemy desires—to deceive us into believing that God loves us so much that He will save us *in* our sin. But whether or not we want to acknowledge it there are consequences for disobedience. And furthermore, when we *choose to continue in sin*—in any aspect of our life—God will not accept us. For example, in response to the children of Israel He stated the following through the prophet Jeremiah:

> "Thus saith the Lord unto this people, Thus have they loved to wander, they have not refrained their feet, *therefore the Lord doth not accept them*; he will now remember their iniquity, and visit their sins" (Jer. 14:10).

It is clear that God will not accept us if we knowingly disobey Him. There are numerous examples in the Bible to support this. For example, in Genesis we are told about our first parent's plight:

> "So he drove out the man; and he placed at the east of the garden of Eden Cherubims, and a flaming sword which turned every way, to keep the way of the tree of life" (Gen. 3:24).

And in the final book of the Bible, Revelation, we are told about the fate of the lost:

> "And whosoever was not found written in the book of life was cast into the lake of fire" (Rev. 20:15).

We Cannot Naturally Choose To Do "Good"

There is another point to consider with this concept of unconditional love and acceptance. The idea that people will eventually do or choose what is right if they are loved unconditionally by God (and others) comes directly from humanistic theory. Specifically, it is based on the notion that we are born with the tendency to do good and that we naturally move toward the positive (remember Carl Rogers and Abraham Maslow?). But such thinking is not in agreement with God's Word. Consider the following verses:

> "…There is none that doeth good, no, not one." (Rom. 3:12)

"...the carnal (or natural) mind is enmity against God; for it is not subject to the law of God, *neither indeed can be."* (Rom. 8:7)

The only way that our carnal minds can change and that we can "do good" is through the power of the Holy Spirit. But it does not stop there. We also have a role in this experience. This is why we are told in *Philippians 2:12, 13* to "...*work out (our) own salvation* with fear and trembling... for it is God which worketh in you both to will and to do of his good pleasure." Paul also tells us that he had to "die daily" (1 Cor. 15:31), and Jesus admonishes us to "*strive* to enter in at the strait gate (Luke 13:24)."

Again, we cannot do any of this on our own, which is why Jesus tells us, "without me ye can do nothing" (John 15:5). But the truth is that there is an effort we must make toward our own salvation. Some refer to this as legalism—it is not. It is the combination of human and divine effort that is necessary in our Christian walk.

Thus, the idea that we will naturally do what God requires if we know we are loved unconditionally is just another deception from the enemy to prevent us from doing our part in the process of salvation.

"Unconditional"—Inadequate to Describe God's Love

The last point that I would like to make about the concept that God's love is unconditional is that the word "unconditional" is truly inadequate to describe God's love. God's love is almost humanly impossible to define or describe. However, there is enough in the Bible that talks about the kind of love He shows toward us that we don't have to look to the philosophies of the world to help us understand it. I like the way the following authors put it:

> "There is a strong temptation to use vocabulary that is popular in society in order to make Christianity sound relevant. Christians have something far better than the world has to offer, but in expressing that good news they confuse people by using words that are already loaded with humanistic connotations and systems of thought. It would be better not to use the expression *unconditional love* when describing God's love. There are plenty of other good words that do not skew His love or character with psychological distortion."[5]

The Prodigal Son: Love and Acceptance Unconditional?

The question may be asked, is not the story of the prodigal son (Luke 15) an example of God's unconditional love and acceptance toward us? Often when this Bible story is told, it is implied that father accepted the son unconditionally. But let us look at this parable more closely. First of all, the son acknowledged his mistake and repented (which could both be viewed as "conditions") before he returned to his father's home. In addition, the father waited for the son to return (another "condition"). As stated by one author:

> "It remains true that the prodigal's son left the pigpen and his sinful life *before* his father took him back. We don't read of the father traveling to the city where his son partied, apologizing for the 'legalistic rules' which drove the son away, then offering the son an unconditional invitation to return, irrespective of how he lived…"[6]

A careful study of this story reveals that it does not condone the humanistic concept of unconditional love. Rather, it is an exhibition of God's forgiveness, grace, and longsuffering patience toward us as human beings.

We Cannot Love Unconditionally!

If we are honest with ourselves, we will admit that unconditional love (between humans) is a myth. Human beings are "naturally self-biased and the human heart is so deceitful that one can fool himself into thinking that he is loving unconditionally, when in fact he has all kinds of conditions."[7]

It is true that we should embrace our fellow brothers and sisters in Christ with love. But we must recognize that sinful, human love can never truly be unconditional. Furthermore, on our own, we cannot love as God would have us. We must first have His love in our hearts, which in turn will give us what we need to truly love each other.

You Can't Judge Me!

Earlier, we talked about the prevailing sentiment that Christians who question their fellow brethren about behavior or lifestyle are judgmental or legalistic. Is this true? Should we leave another Christian to do as he or she pleases in an effort to supposedly reveal the love of God toward him or her? Are we "Pharisaical" when we talk about Biblical standards and encourage others to follow them? This is what is believed by many advocates of the unconditional love/acceptance philosophy. But in order to understand the truth about this issue, we need to look more closely at the concept of "judging."

In Matthew 7:1, Jesus says, "Judge not, that ye be not judged." This, by the way, is a text used by many to support the idea that we should not focus too much on issues such as dress, diet, worship styles, etc. But we must understand that in this verse Jesus is referring "particularly to judging another's motives, not to judging the right or wrong of his acts."[8]

When we talk about lifestyle and standards with other Christians, this is not the same as judging them. The act of judging comes in when we put ourselves in the place of God, determining whether or not others will be saved or lost because of their choices. We can also engage in judging when we decide that we know the motive for an individual's behavior.

If we *truly* love our fellow brothers and sisters in Christ, we will want to help them in any way that we can. This may include talking to them about diet, dress, worship styles and other "hot" topics. If I saw a fellow Christian walking toward a fire or a cliff and he or she was indifferent or oblivious, would I be judging him or her if I warned of the danger that lie ahead?

We must remember that we are not showing "love for one another by allowing that which God condemns."[9] Our love for each other will at times lead us to talk with a brother or sister about areas in which they may be straying from God's Word. The idea that we are "judgmental" or "legalistic" when we do so, especially as related to issues of Christian behavior and doctrines, is a ploy of the enemy to minimize Biblical standards and to prevent us from growing spiritually.

Also, the Bible is replete with examples of individuals who were called by God to speak to individuals, families, and even nations about what God required of them (Elijah, Jeremiah, Isaiah, Hosea, John the Baptist, various disciples...). If we were living during the time of these messengers of God, would we consider them judgmental, legalistic, or as not being "unconditional" in their love toward those with whom they spoke?

In summary, the use of the phrase "unconditional" is replete with problems when we apply it to God's relationship toward us as well as our relationship with one another. Again, on the surface it sounds good, but the humanistic foundation from which it is extracted makes it unsuitable for the Christian's walk with God.

Judgmental Christians: They Are Part of the Problem!

Before ending this chapter, I would be remiss if I did not point out that there are Christians who *are* truly judgmental in their approach to others. This type of attitude has contributed to the readiness of many to accept and promote the humanistic concept of unconditional love.

For example, some well-meaning individuals present their views about Biblical standards of diet, worship and related issues in a very staunch, "un-Christ-like" manner. Such persons may use themselves as "measuring sticks" to dictate to others how they should live their lives. Or they may attempt to take the place of God by condemning (whether it is openly or in their minds) those whose views they believe are not Biblically based.

Those of us who are or have been guilty of this *must* repent and ask the Lord to change our hearts. The fact of the matter is that the Bible says, "Examine *yourselves*, whether ye be in the faith; prove your own selves" (2 Cor. 13:5). This should be our first and foremost concern. It is as we do this in our own lives that we can then be open to the Holy Spirit's leading about when and how we should talk to others when we see them going astray. We should also recognize that it is the work of the Holy Spirit to convict and convert. All we can do is present the issue and then pray for each other.

CHAPTER 8

MEETING NEEDS ATTRACTS AND KEEPS CHURCH MEMBERS, OR DOES IT?

Yet a third humanistic concept that has crept into Christianity is that of "meeting needs." Today's church seems to be on a mission: to meet the needs, physical and emotional, of both current and prospective members. This activity reveals the influence of such humanists as Abraham Maslow who, as indicated in an earlier chapter, contends that human beings are motivated by needs. Although this philosophy sounds well intentioned, does it reflect the true mission of the church?

Felt Needs and the Church

There are many examples of programs and philosophies in our church that seem to reflect this philosophy. Consider the "seeker-sensitive" movement, which targets the "unchurched"—those who are supposedly not interested in, and would typically never attend church. In an attempt to reach this group, churches now offer various types of services and programs, such as day cares, fitness centers, and cafeterias. The idea is that if some of the needs of these individuals can be met by the church, they will more likely attend and eventually join the congregation. This concept is rapidly becoming popular in many Christian circles.

Felt Needs and Worship

Another focal point of the seeker-sensitive movement is the church worship service. It is common for pastors who adhere to the principles of this movement to focus on meeting the needs of their members. Thus, sermons focus more on practical issues such as finances, relationships, and marriage, than on topics such as sin, judgment, repentance or doctrine. Consider the following directive for pastors:

> "Limit your preaching to roughly 20 minutes, because boomers don't have much time to spare. And don't forget to keep your messages light and informal, liberally sprinkling them with humor and personal anecdotes."[1]

This same thinking spills over into the arena of music. Proponents of the seeker-sensitive movement believe that the music used in the worship service should appeal to the needs of the unchurched. Consider the following statement by Rick Warren, pastor of the Saddleback Church in California:

> "We use the style of music the majority of people in our church listen to on the radio. They like bright, happy, cheerful music with a strong beat. Their ears are accustomed to music with a strong bass line and rhythm. For the first time in history, there exists a universal music style that can be heard in every country of the world. It's called contemporary pop/rock."[2]

Felt Needs and Church Programs/Ministries

In addition to targeting the unchurched, this "needs" philosophy has also affected other aspects of church programming. For example, there has been an increase in the number of ministries, committees, and seminars/workshops aimed at meeting some of the non-spiritual needs of church members. These include, but are not limited to, the following:

- Committees that are aimed at making members and visitors feel "welcomed" when they attend church
- Emphasis on social activities for church members (sports activities, church outings, picnics)
- "Ministries" and programs that focus on specific groups, such as unmarried singles, divorcees, and single parents

Those who promote these types of programs and ministries appear to believe that when the non-spiritual needs of members are met they will more likely remain a part of the congregation and take a more active role in their churches. In many cases this does occur—so what, then, is wrong with this philosophy?

What Is the Truth about Meeting Felt Needs?

As with the other humanistic philosophies that have been mentioned, this emphasis on "felt" needs—needs that are obvious and real in the lives of each individual—seems innocuous on the surface. There is some "truth" to the idea that there are non-spiritual needs that must be met in order to help others along the way (remember, the best deception is that which mixes truth and error). If we read the Bible and study the life of Christ, we will discover that He did consider non-spiritual needs when He ministered to others. For example, in the feeding of the 5,000 we are told that Jesus "knew that a tired, hungry throng could not receive spiritual benefit, and he did not forget their bodily needs."[3]

However, when we study God's Word further, it becomes clear that Jesus never catered to the non-spiritual needs of others in a manner that overshadowed his primary goal, to help them to know God and obtain salvation. In addition, Jesus did not in any way downplay the teachings of the Scriptures nor did he utilize any of the methods or teachings of the Greek or Roman culture (the secular society of his day) to win people to God.

Unfortunately, the same cannot be said of those who promote this "needs" philosophy today. Oftentimes, meeting needs has become more important than anything else, including a "thus saith the Lord." In fact, one author states it aptly when he says that in many Christian circles "needs have replaced the commandments…"[4]

Unmet Needs and Spirituality

Another erroneous aspect of this focus on "needs" is the idea that people are more likely to have spiritual problems when they have unmet needs, a concept promoted by many of those who accept this philosophy. If we seriously study Scripture, we will see that needs, as defined by humanistic psychology, were never relevant in helping God's people spiritually.

There are several cases of Biblical characters whose earthly needs were fulfilled yet made poor decisions and were spiritually lacking. One author expounds on this as follows:

> "Many Christians believe the humanistic lie that when people's needs are met, they will be good, loving people. Through the influence of humanistic psychology, they believe that people sin because their needs are not met….However, Scripture does

not bear this out. Adam and Eve had it all. There was no need in their lives that was not being met to its very fullest, and yet they chose to sin, have their own way, disbelieve God, believe a lie, and love self more than God....The Bible places God's will and purpose at the center rather than so-called psychological needs...Throughout the Bible the panorama of God's plan for humanity.... unfolds according to His own will and purpose, which include but go far beyond human need."[5]

If this "needs" philosophy was accurate, then Adam and Eve would never have disobeyed God. As we see, however, this was not the case at all!

Seek God First!

As we consider God's plan for us in His Word, there is little evidence to show that He wants us to spend an inordinate amount of time and attention on meeting our "needs." What He does admonish us to do is to spend more time seeking Him because "....it is Christ that every sinner needs."[6] When we direct our energy toward fulfilling this spiritual need, we become better equipped to overcome the temptations of the enemy.

In addition, when we seek Christ first, every other earthly need that we have will be supplied, according to what God sees is best for our spiritual growth. This is why in Matthew 6:33 Jesus tells us, "seek ye first the kingdom of God, and His righteousness, and *all* these things shall be added unto you."

Interestingly, when we quote this text, there often seems to be a focus on seeking the kingdom of God. But the text also states that we should seek "His righteousness." When we seek God's righteousness, we seek His will, His purpose and His glory. In the pursuit of His kingdom and His righteousness, we will not be too consumed with our physical, social or emotional needs. Paul also tells us, "my God shall supply all your needs according to his riches in glory by Christ Jesus." (Phil. 4:19)

The Scripture is full of examples where the needs of God's people were fulfilled. And when they were not, it was apparent that God was working out His will in their lives. Unfortunately, the majority of Christians do not believe that if we as individuals or a church place our primary focus on spiritual issues, everything else will fall in place. This reflects a lack of faith in God and His Word.

Most of us think we need to do "something," such as implementing many of the strategies and program previously discussed, to attract people to church and keep them there. However, what we do not recognize is that human effort alone cannot solve this issue. It is God's problem. If we would spend more time focusing on following Him, fulfilling His purpose, and giving glory to Him, we would see more people being drawn to the church and staying there!

The "Needs" Focus Encourages Self-Centeredness

Another problem with this emphasis on needs is that it keeps us focused on self, rather than on God. If most of our time is spent on making sure our felt needs are met, how can we follow the Biblical instruction to deny self and the desires of the flesh? This undue emphasis on needs also encourages us to look to God as some type of "candy man" who will give us what we need whenever we want it. The following statement summarizes it well:

> "....The Christian church, traditionally keen on mortifying the desires of the flesh, on crucifying the needs of the self in pursuit of the religious life, has eagerly adopted the language of needs for itself...we now hear that 'Jesus will meet your every need,' as though He was some kind of divine psychiatrist or divine detergent, as though God were simply to service us."[7]

This philosophy that God will "meet our needs" is increasingly being promoted among Christians. I have become almost sick as I witness the number of sermons and songs focusing almost exclusively on what God will do for us when we are in need (not necessarily referring to spiritual needs). This view of God prevents us from developing the type of relationship He would like for us to have with Him—one in which we love and obey Him and not merely look to Him for what we can "get" from Him.

A Spiritual Danger Zone!

This undue emphasis on meeting needs is dangerous to our spiritual growth. Any time we invent methods for reaching people that are man-centered or encourage people to view God primarily as someone who will fulfill their desires or wants, we do not lead individuals to God, but away from Him. This may not be evident at first, but as time passes, it becomes increasingly clear (to those who are students of the Scriptures) that the people who are won by these methods seem to have a weak, self-centered type of religious experience. As stated by one pastor, "it is difficult to see how one can begin with the glory of man or self—including 'felt needs'—and progress to the glory of God."[8]

Much more can be said about the dangers inherent in this "needs" focus among Christians. Many are drawn to the idea of meeting needs because, on the surface, it seems effective. For example, most mega-churches and outwardly successful ministers appear to strongly promote this philosophy. As a result, large numbers are drawn to such churches or individuals. But it takes faith in God to believe His Word and seek His will as we address problems in our lives and in the Christian church. That is why the apostle Paul states, "without faith it is impossible to please him" (Heb. 11:6). The true believer will exemplify this kind of faith and will not look to the wisdom of man for help, even if the results look good. Remember, "we walk by faith, not by sight" (2 Cor. 5:7).

CHAPTER 9

EMOTIONS—WHAT DO I DO WITH THEM AS A CHRISTIAN?

Psychologists and other mental health professionals consider emotions to be a critical aspect of human functioning. Because of this, I thought it would be important to include a chapter on this issue and explore the impact of the secular psychological view of emotions on Christianity.

Are Emotions Important?

During my psychology training, I was taught that it is important to understand, accept, and express emotions in order to be psychologically healthy. Most mental health professionals hold this same belief.

The thinking behind this concept is that when we repress or purposely try to hide our feelings, this leads to psychological problems. In order to resolve such difficulties, a person must identify and accept his or her emotions and also learn how to express them in a "healthy" manner.

According to those in the mental health field, this can be done with the help of a mental health professional, such as a psychologist. Or, as is often the case nowadays, individuals may seek help for their emotions by reading information available to them through a self-help book, workshop/seminar, or even the television.

Should Christians Ignore Emotions?

The answer is a resounding no! It is clear that feelings are an important part of our human lives. We were obviously created to experience certain emotions. In fact, the Bible is full of examples where God the Father and the Son exhibited feelings such as anger, compassion, and sadness (Exod. 4:14, 2 Chron. 36:15, Matt. 9:36, Luke 19:41).

It is also clear that our emotions can have an impact on our overall functioning. According to Solomon,

"A *merry heart* doeth good like a medicine, but a *broken spirit* drieth the bones" (Prov. 17:22).

"A sound heart is the life of the flesh: but *envy* the rottenness of the bones" (Prov. 14:30).

In addition to this, we must recognize that emotions are often like "warning lights on the dashboard of the car... which signal that something is wrong under the hood..."[1] When we experience emotions, especially negative ones, we know that something is wrong and must be addressed. Thus, we cannot ignore emotions and need to recognize that they can play a central role in our lives.

How Should Christians Handle Emotions?

Even though we can't ignore emotions, we must be aware that the view of emotions held by those in clinical/counseling psychology differs from that which is revealed in God's Word. For the most part, secular psychologists encourage people to spend an inordinate amount of time examining and analyzing their feelings. It is believed that engaging in this process can help us better understand and cope with problems.

However, the spiritual danger to this perspective on emotions is that it encourages individuals to focus too much on self, contrary to God's admonition to deny self. This philosophy can also lead us away from a dependence on Him. This is likely why we are told that, "it is not wise to look to ourselves and study our emotions....we are to look away from self to Jesus."[2]

Some Christians attempt to use the Bible to support secular psychology's view of emotions. For example, I recently attended a religious seminar where a member of the audience stated that the Bible says, "examine yourselves..." (2 Cor. 13:5). This person then proceeded to use this text to support the idea that we should study and understand our feelings. But is this a correct interpretation of this Scripture?

The servant of the Lord comments on this text as follows:

"Some conscientious souls, on reading this (2 Cor. 13:5), immediately begin to criticize their every feeling and emotion. *But this is not correct self-examination.* It is not the petty feelings and emotions that are to be examined. The life, the character, is to be measured by the only standard of character, God's holy law. "[3]

This quotation highlights the fact that self-examination is a spiritual process that helps us in determining how well our lives line up with God's Word. This clearly differs from the self-focused investigation of emotions encouraged by those in secular psychology.

If we study the Bible, we can find no example of God asking His people to examine and seek to understand their emotions to deal with their problems. His goal was to encourage them to turn to Him, not to self, for help.

What About Anger?

Another area in which Christians attempt to use the Bible to support this focus on emotions is with the issue of anger. Psychologists, for the most part, believe that anger is at the root of many problems; in some cases this is true. For example, there is evidence that anger or hostility can contribute to various health issues. [4, 5, 6]

To resolve these and other difficulties that result from anger, those who adhere to secular psychological principles claim that anger should be acknowledged and expressed. Christians who agree with this idea tend to support such thinking with Bible verses such as Ephesians 4:26, which states, "Be ye angry, and sin not." Such individuals interpret this to mean that God permits or even commands us to feel angry, as long as we don't "sin" in the way we handle this anger.

However, consider the following commentary on this verse:

> "The anger here spoken of (is) a righteous indignation...
> Righteous indignation has a most important function in stimulating men in the battle against evil. Jesus was not angered at any personal affront, but by hypocritical challenges to God, and injustices done to others (see Mark 3:5). Justifiable anger is directed against the wrong act without animosity toward the wrongdoer. To be able to separate the two is a supremely great Christian achievement."[7]

To reiterate, Jesus was angered only when there were *hypocritical challenges to God* and *injustices toward others*. He did not get angry when He was personally treated unfairly or insulted. In fact, there is no Scriptural evidence to suggest that God ever encouraged or condoned the display of anger for self-centered reasons. However, when we consider secular psychology, most of the focus has to do with anger that results from being personally injured, mistreated, or insulted. The thinking is that human beings should be encouraged to accept and express such anger to resolve their problems.

For example, in a book addressed to survivors of sexual abuse, the authors make the following comments to those who have been abused:

> "You may dream of murder or castration (referring to those who abused them). It can be pleasurable to fantasize such scenes in vivid detail... Let yourself imagine it to your heart's content."[8]

> "You may want to see them (the perpetrators) suffer. You may want revenge. Be clear that whatever you do, you are doing it for yourself."[9]

The promotion of this type of anger is in direct opposition to God's Word and His character. In fact, God's response to the anger that results from personal injury or mistreatment is revealed in the following verses:

> "But now ye also put off all these; anger, wrath, malice, blasphemy, filthy communication out of your mouth" (Col. 3:8).

> "Let all bitterness, and wrath, and anger, and clamour, and evil speaking, be put away from you, with all malice: And be ye kind one to another, tenderhearted, forgiving one another, even as God for Christ's sake hath forgiven you" (Eph. 4: 31, 32).

> "But I say unto you, Love your enemies, bless them that curse you, do good to them that hate you, and pray for them which despitefully use you, and persecute you" (Matt. 5:44).

These and other principles in God's Word tell us that we must put away or "put off" anger—not talk about it, accept it, express it, or even fantasize about it. To further emphasize, we are admonished that "wrong dispositions and feelings are to be rooted out."[10]

And as stated above, for those who have hurt us, we must pray for and forgive them. Of course, it is humanly impossible to deal with mistreatment in this way. We can do this only as we rely on God to give us His power, through the Holy Spirit—and He will, if we ask Him.

More Evidence: A Secular Perspective on Anger

There are some in the field of psychology who recognize that the expression of anger is not helpful and can be even hurtful. Consider the following:

> "The evidence dictates now that it is unintelligent to encourage persons to be aggressive." [11]

> "The psychological rationale for ventilating anger does not stand up under experimental scrutiny. The weight of the evidence indicates precisely the opposite: Expressing anger makes you angrier, solidifies an angry attitude, and establishes a hostile habit." [12]

> "Most research now says that catharsis—'letting it all out'—isn't helpful and may increase a person's hostility, according to a 1999 study by psychologist Brad Bushman."[13]

These authors, who do not proclaim any religious beliefs or affiliation, seem to support what God says in His Word. The expression of anger is not good for us—from either a spiritual or an emotional perspective. Thus, would it not be wise for those who have ascribed to the popular views on anger to reconsider their position?

What About Guilt?

Another specific emotion to consider as related to secular psychology and Christianity is guilt. Many psychology experts believe that, for the most part, guilt is something that is unhealthy and should be avoided. Consider the following quotes:

> "Guilt is the worse experience known to humans. It... makes you feel unworthy and miserable... It is caused by

thinking you have done something wrong... you are taught to feel guilt when someone judges you—about anything—how you dress, how you think, what you do.... There is no right or wrong, only experience to learn from. So get out there and en-joy learning and living and growing. Toss guilt out."[14]

"Guilt is not natural behavior.... (Guilt) is a convenient tool for manipulation.... a futile waste of time."[15]

These quotes not only reflect the thinking of many secular psychologists, but also of a large number of Christians. For exam-ple, the idea is often promoted that people should not be led to feel "guilty" or "bad" when they attend church. This has had an impact on various facets of the church, such as the worship service. (As a side note, isn't it interesting to see how the concepts of secular psychology have affected worship in so many different ways?)

The goal of many churches these days is to structure the ser-vice in a manner that will help the members feel "good." This often includes, but is not limited to the use of upbeat music, dra-ma, liturgical dance, pantomimes, etc. This thinking has also had a significant impact on the sermons that are preached. It is rare, now, to go to any church (Adventist or non-Adventist) and hear a pastor preaching on topics such as sin, judgment, or repentance. The issue of sin is avoided so much that even some in the secular world are recognizing this.

Consider the following words of a psychiatrist:

"Where, indeed, did sin go? What became of it...This very word 'sin'... seems to have disappeared...It was once a strong word...It described a central point in every civilized human being's life plan and lifestyle. But the word went away. It has almost disappeared–the word along with the notion."[16]

In our efforts to ensure that we don't feel guilty, we have al-most completely eradicated the focus on sin, individually and cor-porately as a church. But this is not congruent with God's Word: "For all have sinned, and come short of the glory of God" (Rom. 3:23). When we acknowledge that we have sinned before God, through the conviction of the Holy Spirit, we *will* experience a sense of guilt.

As we recognize the separation from God that results from a sinful act, look or thought, this should drive us to Jesus, our

Savior, who is our advocate before God (1 John 2:1). When we go to Him and confess and repent of our sin, He will then forgive us and cleanse us from "all unrighteousness" (1 John 1:9). It is only when we experience this that we will be able to rid ourselves of guilty feelings.

Guilt should not be avoided. In fact, those who don't feel guilt are spiritually dead. It is like a person with leprosy; individuals with this disease lose the ability to feel pain because nerve endings become dead. This can lead to their hurting themselves because they lack that "signal" (pain) to warn them of danger. Guilt is a signal or a God-given "alarm system" to alert us to the dangers of sin. Without guilt, we would not be able to know when there is something spiritually wrong in our lives that needs to be addressed. Thus, the experience of guilt is critical in our lives as Christians and plays an important role in our salvation.

When Guilt is Damaging

It is important to recognize that in the Christian experience, not all guilt is beneficial. There are two types of guilt: that which leads us to Christ to confess and repent of our sin, and the other, which leads us to self-condemnation and feelings of hopelessness.

Consider the lives of Peter and Judas. Peter experienced guilt when he denied Christ, and this led to his repentance and ultimate conversion. On the other hand, the guilt that Judas experienced led to his ultimate death (suicide). This is why the Bible states that "godly sorrow [as exhibited by Peter] worketh repentance to salvation not to be repented of; but the sorrow of the world [as exhibited by Judas] worketh death" (2 Cor. 7:10).

Thus, it is important for us to pray for that "godly sorrow" for ourselves and others as we are faced with our sin. This comes only through the conviction of the Holy Spirit, who leads and guides us into all truth.

In summary, guilt is an integral part of the process of the Christian life. Most psychologists tell us differently because they do not acknowledge the role of sin in our lives. Satan knows this and has led many to accept the false teachings about guilt and sin. But as Christians we cannot ignore either. Our acknowledgement of sin leads us to guilt, which leads to the Savior, and it is only through Him that we can be saved.

CHAPTER 10

I'M A CHRISTIAN, BUT I STILL NEED PSYCHOTHERAPY!

When I first started working as a therapist, it was very common for Christians who came to my office to make statements such as, "As a Christian, I should be able to get the help I need from God through prayer and the study of His Word. I feel ashamed that I have to seek therapy."

Over the years, this has changed. Specifically, I have witnessed Christians becoming more comfortable with using therapy to address emotional or interpersonal problems. Many of these individuals assure me that they have a close relationship with God. However, their belief seems to be that God speaks through people, which includes psychologists or other therapists.

For most of my professional life, I viewed this as a positive step on the part of Christians. I would often congratulate these persons for their "openness" to therapy. The rationale I used for this thinking was that just as people with physical problems need the help of a physician, so those with mental or emotional problems need the help of a therapist.

Many Christians, both lay and professional, now hold this view. As a result, we have seen an exponential growth in the number of Christians seeking psychotherapy.

As anyone reading this book has probably guessed, I no longer hold these beliefs. Some of the reasons for my change of viewpoint are based on the information presented in previous chapters on therapy that focuses on childhood experiences. In addition to this, there are other aspects of traditional psychotherapy that have caused me to now view it with "caution," especially as a Christian. I would now like to present some of these concerns.

What is the Goal of Psychotherapy?

Psychotherapy is defined as the "treatment of mental and emotional disorders through the use of psychological techniques designed to encourage communication of conflicts and insight into problems, with the goal being relief of symptoms and changes in behavior leading to improved social and vocational functioning, and personality growth."[1]

In short, psychotherapy seeks to improve the lives of individuals by encouraging them to communicate (or talk) about and gain an understanding of their inner conflicts (such as thoughts and feelings).

Based on my experience, I can say that there is some partial truth to the idea that talking about a problem can increase understanding. And, in some cases, it may even contribute to resolution of the problematic issue.

For example, I have witnessed cases in which various symptoms, such as poor appetite, aggressive and angry behaviors, insomnia, or sadness were alleviated after clients shared their inmost feelings and thoughts and gained some understanding of people and situations that were contributing to their difficulties. If this is true, then, shouldn't Christians be encouraged to seek help from psychotherapists?

Christians and Psychotherapy: Beware!

As Christians, we must remember that there are many worldly methods that may appear to "work," so to speak, but have the potential to be spiritually dangerous. Could this be the case with therapy? What concerns, if any, should Christians have about seeking psychotherapy?

As a psychologist I have observed that the relief that many gain through therapy is often temporary. Because we are living in a world of sin, difficulties will arise. However, instead of turning to God, more and more Christians are turning to therapists for answers. Some even find themselves re-cycling in and out of therapy whenever they can't cope with their problems. This can create a dependence on therapy, similar to dependence on drugs (legal or illegal) for relief of physical or emotional symptoms. This is dangerous. Why? Because it is the "essential role of every Christian…to learn complete dependence upon Christ and not upon man."[2] This is why the Bible says, "Cursed be the man that trusteth in man, and maketh flesh his arm" (Jer. 17:5).

The truth is that *any* help that is *solely* dependent on what a human being can do is limited in its scope. Of all people, Christians need to come to the place where they believe that only God can provide the complete and lasting solution to their problems.

But Pain and Suffering Hurt!

There are times, however, when we may turn to God and He does not provide immediate answers or relief. What should be the Christian's response?

The philosophy of the secular world is that human beings cannot tolerate the emotional pain and suffering that often accompany the problems of life. Thus, we are encouraged to seek "symptom relief," which includes entertainment, drugs, alcohol, and, yes, *psychotherapy* (remember, one part of the aforementioned definition of psychotherapy is that it seeks to relieve "symptoms").

However, the Christian way should be different. God's Word tells us that He often allows difficulties in our lives to help us grow spiritually. For example, He says:

> "Now no chastening for the present seemeth to be joyous, but grievous: nevertheless afterward it yieldeth the peaceable fruit of righteousness unto them which are exercised thereby" (Heb. 12:11).

> "...My son, despise not thou the chastening of the Lord; nor faint when thou art rebuked of him: For whom the Lord loveth he chasteneth, and scourgeth every son whom he receiveth" (Heb. 12:5, 6).

> "Beloved, think it not strange concerning the fiery trial which is to try you, as though some strange thing happened unto you: but rejoice, inasmuch as ye are partakers of Christ's sufferings; that, when his glory shall be revealed, ye may be glad also with exceeding joy" (1 Peter 4:12, 13).

These verses indicate that there is a spiritual purpose to trials and suffering. This is evident as we look through Scripture and see numerous examples of how God used affliction for the good of His people. Trials can:

- Bring us closer to God
- Help us discover traits of character that we need to change (through His power)
- Teach us not to repeat mistakes
- Help us develop a stronger faith in God
- Help us become more compassionate and understanding toward others
- Teach us to be more obedient to God[3]

Given the spiritual benefits, so to speak, of trials, when a Christian goes to a therapist for "relief," how does this affect him or her, in the long run? Could it be that psychotherapy can actually impede our spiritual growth? I think it can and that for many Christians it has.

Christ Our Example

Christians are named as such because they consider themselves to be followers of Christ. He is our example and when we look at His life, we can see that He did not seek human relief from trials. Christ was "despised and rejected of men; a man of sorrows, and acquainted with grief" (Isa. 53:3).

In that same chapter we are also told, "He was oppressed, and he was afflicted, yet he opened not his mouth" (Isa. 53:7). The apostle Paul adds that Christ "learned...obedience by the things which he suffered" (Heb. 5:8). These and many other passages reveal that Christ understood the purpose of suffering. He trusted His Father and his response was ever to be "nevertheless not my will, but thine, be done" (Luke 22:42).

Many of us have been so indoctrinated by the idea that we should turn to counselors for help that this perspective on trials, pain, and suffering, may sound strange, even crazy! Some may view me as harsh, unsympathetic, and uncaring because of what I have shared.

But such thinking reflects how far we as Christians have come from relying on God and His Word in our lives. It will take a complete re-education, through the Holy Spirit regenerating and renewing our minds, to grasp and apply these principles.

Can I Do What Christ Did?

Some may be saying, "Well, Christ was able to cope with trials in this way because He was God." In response, the Bible tells us that Christ "took not on him the nature of angels; but he took on him the seed of Abraham. Wherefore in *all* things it behooved him to be made like unto his brethren (the human race)" (Heb. 2:16, 17). Christ could not have been our example if He did not become as one of us. There is nothing we have been called to endure that He did not endure, for He was "in all points tempted like as we are, yet without sin" (Heb. 4:15).

Christ depended on His Father for help as He lived on this earth. We are to do the same. Yes, it is *humanly impossible* for us to respond to difficulties, to pain and suffering, as instructed by the Word of God. But through the power of the Holy Spirit we can do all things through Christ who strengthens us (Phil. 4:13). We must learn to trust God's Word and believe that whatever He commands, He gives strength to fulfill.

Should Christians Ever Turn to Others for Emotional Support?

In spite of all that I have stated thus far, it is important for readers to understand one thing. There are times when it may help to talk to someone when we are experiencing difficulties. Sometimes a godly friend, church member, church leader, or family member can provide encouragement and spiritual guidance. Seeking support from godly Christians we trust and respect does not mean that our faith is weak or that we are lacking spiritually. Even Christ sometimes looked to the disciples for support—when he was in the Garden of Gethsemane, for example.

The danger exists when we become *dependent* on these individuals, especially therapists, for relief from our pain and, risk missing out on the spiritual growth that comes from trusting in God for help at these times.

Behavior Change and Therapy

Some individuals may be asking, What about therapy that focuses on changing behavior and not merely relieving symptoms? There are many psychologists who spend minimal time talking about childhood or helping people momentarily "feel" better. These mental health professionals may focus more on behavior change, one of the goals of therapy cited earlier in this chapter. The basis of their work is rooted in behaviorism, one of three major perspectives (outside of the psychodynamic and humanistic approaches) in clinical/counseling psychology.

Briefly, the behavioristic approach is based on the idea that what we do is the ultimate test of who we are.[4] According to this theory, the behaviors that we engage in are based on rewards or punishments that we experience. For example, we may not drive too fast because we fear getting a ticket (punishment). Or, we may work hard at a job in order that we can be promoted (rewards).

Is Anything Wrong with Seeking Behavior Therapy?

One outgrowth of behaviorism is behavior therapy, which involves the use of "specific techniques that employ psychological principles to constructively change human behavior."[5] This type of therapy has been used to treat various problem behaviors such as smoking, overeating, impulsivity, and aggressive behavior, to name a few.

In general, behavior therapy has been found to be helpful for decreasing negative, unhealthy behaviors and increasing positive, healthy behaviors. On the surface, this type of psychological treatment does not appear to be in direct conflict with God's Word because the Christian life does require behavior change.

However, the danger of relying on behavior change *alone* is that such change does not address the "heart." Psychology cannot change the heart. But the gospel can, because through the power of the Holy Spirit, it transforms us from within.

This is what Jesus meant when he told Nicodemus "Ye must be born again" (John 3:7). Nicodemus was a Pharisee, and Pharisees were known for focusing on changing outward behavior while neglecting to seek inward change. Those who rely heavily on behavior therapy are, on another level, also guilty of this Pharisaical practice. This is evident when we consider that this form of therapy addresses only the outside, *behavior,* and does not get to the root, *the heart.*

It is also important to mention that most psychologists with a behaviorist perspective do not acknowledge the need for a power outside of what human beings can do for themselves. These individuals tend to believe that man can remedy his own problems.

Thus, the goal is to teach people how they can enhance their lives by changing their behavior—*without God's power*. What many Christians do not realize is that when they rely *solely* on therapists for behavior change, they are also denying the need for God's power in their lives.

But true healing comes only when we ask God to change our hearts, including our desires, thoughts, motivations, and feelings. It is when we experience this heart work that genuine behavior change will follow and it will be a change that will last!

The Case Against Psychotherapy: A Secular View

Over the years there have been some "lone voices" in the secular world that have openly expressed skepticism regarding psychotherapy. One such person is Dr. Tana Dineen, a psychologist who gave up her clinical practice. In her book *Manufacturing Victims*, Dr. Dineen describes psychology (specifically, in the clinical/counseling arena) as "an industry focused on self-interest and propelled by financial incentives."[6] If one considers the cost of a psychotherapy session, which can range anywhere from $50 to $150 per hour, it is clear that finances play a major role in the psychological treatment arena. Dr. Tineen also points out that the role of psychology is to "categorize people in…debilitating ways and turn them into victims and thus, "patients," and that psychologists "now translate all of life into a myriad of abuses, addictions, and traumas."[7]

There are a few other individuals who have been courageous enough to question the usefulness of psychotherapy. Some, who are researchers, question the reliability of studies that reportedly confirm the effectiveness of therapy.[8] Others purport that society has been brainwashed by the psychology industry and even proclaim that it has made us more helpless in dealing with life's problems.[9, 10]

It is true that those who express skepticism about psychotherapy are a minority compared to those who believe in its effectiveness. However, as Christians, we should be careful never to base our decision on the majority. Our guide is the "law and the testimony." When secular experts conflict with God's Word, we are not to give heed to their opinions (or even their research). However, when the secular world "speaks" according to a "thus saith the Lord," we can know that they are confirming what we know is truth.

Before ending this chapter, I must state that there are many mental health professionals who sincerely believe they are helping others by providing psychotherapy treatment. The goal is not to denigrate these individuals or question their motives. By pointing out the dangers of psychotherapy as well as questioning its effectiveness, it is my prayer that laypeople and therapists who are Christians will begin to look more closely at this issue. It is also the hope that they will pray for guidance and direction from the Holy Spirit as they contemplate the information that is presented.

CHAPTER 11

CHRISTIAN PSYCHOLOGY: IT'S MORE SAFE, ISN'T IT?

Many Christians are aware of some of the dangers of secular psychology. Thus, when they decide to seek therapy, special efforts are made to find a "Christian" therapist. Personally, I used to advertise myself as a "Christian psychologist." But, what did this mean?

Basically, I identified myself as a Christian and referred to God and, *sometimes* used the Bible as I provided treatment. However, to be honest, I still continued to apply many of the concepts I learned from Sigmund Freud, Carl Rogers, Abraham Maslow and a host of other secular psychologists. At times, I would even look to the Scriptures to try to support the thinking of secular psychologists and felt that this confirmed my belief in their theories.

Thus, I was still using a "secular" approach to treating my client's difficulties. I would dare say that this is the case with most Christian psychologists or therapists. In fact, one author points out that the Christian Association for Psychological Studies, an organization of psychologists who state they are Christians, admitted the following at one of their meetings:

> "We are often asked if we are 'Christian psychologists' and find it difficult to answer since we don't know what the question implies. We are Christians who are psychologists but at the present time there is no acceptable Christian psychology that is markedly different from non-Christian psychology. It is difficult to imply that we function in a manner that is fundamentally distinct from our non-Christian colleagues. ...as yet there is not an acceptable theory, mode of treatment or research methodology that is distinctly Christian."[1]

What can be concluded from this comment, and from my own experience, is that most therapists who place the word "Christian" before their titles are actually just professing Christians who believe in God and may even utilize Scriptures. However, most of their work is still tainted with secular psychology. Thus, a person who feels safe in going to a Christian therapist may need to think again!

Is Counseling Wrong for Christians?

Before answering this question, it is important to recognize that, technically, there is a difference between counseling and psychotherapy. Psychotherapy typically involves the systematic application of psychological techniques to gain insight, change behavior, etc. Counseling may also involve the use of psychological techniques. But in general, those who truly "counsel" others generally focus on giving advice, guidance, or support on specific life concerns or issues.

With this understanding, my answer to the question about whether counseling is wrong for Christians is no. For example, the wise man Solomon tells us, "in multitude of counselors there is safety" (Prov. 24:6). As one pastor stated, "We often need the wise counsel of others, especially those who are mature in the faith."[2]

The Christian counselor who points those in need of help to Jesus, the true "Counselor," and relies on Biblical principles and, for Seventh-day Adventists, the Spirit of Prophecy, to provide counsel can prove a blessing to many. This type of counseling, however, is one that should deviate from traditional therapy in several ways.

For example, it does not require a large number of counseling meetings or sessions to get to the root of a particular problem. Individuals who provide such counsel do not need any type of psychological or therapy training. It discourages the person from focusing on and relying on "self" to deal with any difficulties he or she may be facing. And it is one in which the counselor encourages the person to not depend on him or her for help, but on God.

An example of this type of counseling is illustrated in an article by the late Mervyn Maxwell, a Seventh-day Adventist theologian and teacher. Dr. Maxwell related the story of a woman who got involved in focusing on "wounds" from her childhood, through reading books, attending workshops, and getting into therapy. She began to develop negative feelings toward her father and her husband. Eventually, she and her husband met with a pastor who used the Scriptures to provide counsel, and she says the following:

"...Pastor Cliff introduced us to Jesus, and *our lives were changed overnight.* Some of you remember the change. I began to remember what it was like when I first accepted Christ—how free, how clean, I felt. I remembered the joy Walt (her husband) and I had shared, and I wanted that again."[3]

What a testimony to the power of God! Only counseling that points people to Him can effectively address human problems and difficulties. If more Christians would believe this and seek Godly wisdom and counsel, there would be no need for them to turn to secular psychology.

CHAPTER 12

WHERE DO WE GO FROM HERE?

Throughout this book, I have presented many of the problems that arise when Christians turn to the deceptive ideas of clinical/counseling psychology for help in the church and in their personal lives. I am sure that some of what has been shared has been a "hard pill to swallow" for many. Unfortunately, most Christians are so influenced by the concepts of secular psychology that the thought of separating from them seems far-fetched.

On a personal level, I know that this is true. I remember how difficult it was for me, as a trained psychologist, to discover that I had to "unlearn" many of those concepts that I had taught and lived by for years. But as I have continued to study and pray for God's guidance, this process has become increasingly easy.

So where do we go from here? How can we address the myriad of difficulties we face in the church and in our lives as Christians? The answer: We must turn back to God, as revealed in His Word and in the gospel of Jesus Christ.

The True Remedy Comes from God

Some may be asking, what does this mean and how can it help me? For others, this may sound too simple or even antiquated. However, the bottom line is that accepting this truth requires faith. The Bible tells us, "without faith it is impossible to please him (God): for he that cometh to God must believe that he is, and that he is a rewarder of them that diligently seek him" (Heb. 11:6).

Most Christians do not have this type of faith. When faced with emotional, mental, or social problems we do not believe that through God's Word and a total surrender to Christ we can have victory in these areas. But whether or not we believe, the fact remains that God has the only true remedy for all the difficulties that plague us, as a church and as individuals.

How can we get the help we need from God? To be honest, this is something that I am still learning. I don't claim to have all

61

the answers. But God has been leading me step by step, and as He unfolds to me the power of His Word and of the gospel, I can more clearly see that He is the answer to all our problems and difficulties!

I would like to share with you some of what I have learned. I am sure there is far more than what will be presented in these next few pages. This is why I strongly encourage each reader to ask God for guidance and direction through His Word so that He will continue to unfold His wisdom and lead us into all truth as we seek His will and His way on these issues.

The Church Today: "Form" Versus "Power"

Earlier we talked about how the concepts of clinical/counseling psychology have made their way into the corporate church and have been utilized to supposedly address many of the issues that are faced by ministers and their congregations. A myriad of techniques and approaches, which include new worship styles, ministries and departments, and even sermons, have been developed on the basis of principles of secular psychology. Many sincere people who accept these methods are not aware of their secular roots, so to speak.

If you were to ask such individuals if these ideas or programs are successful, they would likely answer yes. Typically, to support this response they would point to factors such as the number of people who attend a church, the extent to which young people may be involved, the friendliness of a church, the appeal of the worship service, the number of baptisms, etc. But, are these outcomes truly indicative of success? I don't think so.

Even if a church appears successful, there may still be a lack in a crucial area—spiritual power. Paul sums this up when he states that in the last days many Christians would have "a form of godliness, but (will be) denying the power thereof" (2 Tim. 3:5).

A form of godliness refers to the "external characteristics of religion... (but) the power thereof is that power of God which co-operates with the will of man for the eradication of all sinful tendencies."[1] There may be outward evidence of success with these "new" methods. However, if leaders *and* individual members are not growing in Christ—displaying more of His character and obtaining more victories in the fight against sin—then we can almost be assured that there is more "form" and little to no "power."

Forsaking God's Truth

In Jeremiah 2:13, God reproved His professed people, the Israelites, for committing "two evils." He stated, "they have forsaken me the fountain of living waters, *and* hewed them out cisterns, broken cisterns, that can hold no water."

Unfortunately, many of us as Christians, God's professed people for these times, are guilty of the same. We have forsaken God by turning away from His Word and looking instead to the "broken cisterns" of the philosophies and concepts of secular psychology. These cisterns cannot hold water—they can never be filled. Thus, we can never be satisfied when we use them in place of what God has for us.

The only answer is to turn back to the fountain of living waters—God's truth as given in His Word.

The Example of The Early Christian Church

What would happen if as a corporate church we truly followed God's Word and didn't turn to worldly wisdom and philosophies? One way to answer this question is to study the early Christian church.

The Book of Acts reveals a number of factors that contributed to the growth and effectiveness of the church. First of all, the Bible is clear that it was the Holy Spirit that gave the power that was needed to propel the work during this time. In order for the apostles to receive the power of the Holy Spirit on the day of Pentecost, we are told that they were of "one accord" (Acts 2:1).

> "Before the day of Pentecost they met together and put away all differences. They were of one accord. They believed Christ's promise that the blessing would be given, and they prayed in faith. They did not ask for a blessing for themselves merely; they were weighted with the burden for the salvation of souls."[2]

It should be noted that the Spirit wasn't poured out after an exciting or emotional church service. It came as a result of the disciples putting away their differences, praying in faith, and being more concerned about saving souls than fulfilling their own needs.

As we read further in Acts, we see the results of the outpouring of the Holy Spirit. Peter preached with power about Christ as the Messiah. He spoke about His crucifixion, His resurrection, His ascension to heaven (Acts 2: 22–36). The servant of the Lord states that "the people were made to see themselves as they were, sinful and polluted, and Christ as their Friend and Redeemer."[3] Obviously, no attempt was made to prevent the people from feeling guilty! In addition, there was no effort put forth to boost the listeners' self-esteem or to help them feel "unconditionally accepted."

Also, as far as is known, there was probably no music played— a testimony as to what mere preaching can do! Those who heard this message were convicted and Peter instructed them to "repent, and be baptized" (Acts 2:38). What were the results? On that day, about three thousand souls joined the church!

And what kept them in the church? In the same chapter of Acts, several specific things are revealed:

- "They continued stedfastly in the apostles' doctrine and fellowship, and in breaking of bread, and in prayers" (verse 42)
- "All that believed were together, and had all things common" (verse 44))
- They "sold their possessions and goods, and parted them to all men, as every man had need" (verse 45)
- They continued "daily with one accord in the temple, and breaking bread from house to house, did eat their meat with gladness and singleness of heart" (verse 46)
- And they engaged in "praising God, and having favor with all the people" (verse 47).

The rest of the Book of Acts is filled with examples of the powerful works exhibited by the leaders, and even some of the members, of the church at that time. In spite of the opposition and persecution they experienced, these workers for God, filled with His Spirit, were enabled to preach, teach, and heal, and the church grew exponentially!

What can we learn from the experience of the early church? Simply, there is power in the gospel. If we would preach Christ, His life, death, resurrection, and mediation, we would see similar results today. We don't need all the philosophies and practices that come from secular psychology to attract and keep people in church. It is true that those churches that seek to follow God's Word may not draw the large mega-church crowds. However, God never used numbers to define success—the Bible is clear on this. What He desires is to have people who will be faithful to Him, and seek His will and way in their lives.

The Power of the Gospel

I would like to say a little more about the "power" of the gospel. Paul tells us in Romans 1:16 that he is "not ashamed of the gospel of Christ: for it is the *power* of God unto salvation to *everyone* that believeth." Unfortunately, most Christians, have never experienced this power. The enemy of our souls has done whatever he can to prevent this.

It is through the gospel, the good news that Christ came to this earth to provide forgiveness and restoration to God's image, that lives have and can be changed. When by faith we accept what Christ has done (and is doing) for us, repent of our sins, and continually submit our lives to Him, we will be changed. We will have new thoughts, new feelings, new desires, and even new motives. This experience will renew and revive the body of Christ. It will also help us cope with whatever trial, temptation, or difficult situation that comes our way.

The Bible and Psychology

We are told, "the true principles of psychology are found in the Holy Scriptures."[4] God, our Creator, understands us more than secular psychologists can or ever will. As with the mechanic who knows how to repair a car, He knows what is needed to repair our problems. And He has delineated this in His "manual," the Bible.

There are numerous examples of true psychology principles in God's Word that we can use to address specific concerns. Here are some of them:

For depressed feelings:

> "A merry heart doeth good like a medicine: but a broken spirit drieth the bones" (Prov. 17:22)

> "Finally, brethren, whatsoever things are true, whatsoever things are honest, whatsoever things are just, whatsoever things are pure, whatsoever things are lovely, whatsoever things are of good report; if there be any virtue, and if there be any praise, think on these things" (Phil. 4:8).

For anxiety and worry:

> "Thou wilt keep him in perfect peace, whose mind is stayed on thee: because he trusteth in thee" (Isa. 26:3).

> "These things I have spoken unto you, that in me ye might have peace. In the world ye shall have tribulation: but be of good cheer; I have overcome the world" (John 16:33).

For parenting concerns:

> "And, ye fathers, provoke not your children to wrath: but bring them up in the nurture and admonition of the Lord" (Eph. 6:4).

> "Train up a child in the way he should go: and when he is old, he will not depart from it" (Prov. 22:6).

For anger:

> "A soft answer turneth away wrath" (Prov. 15:1).

For a better attitude:

> "Let this mind be in you, which was also in Christ Jesus" (Phil. 2:5).

These verses just scratch the surface of what we can find in God's Word. Unfortunately, many Christians view secular psychology as more practical than the Bible. I have heard many say that the Bible is not relevant and does not address most contemporary concerns. What they fail to understand is that without the Holy Spirit, we cannot gain much, if any, benefit from the Scriptures.

It is the Spirit that gives us the wisdom and power to understand and apply the principles of God's Word. If we will ask, the

Holy Spirit will lead and guide us into all truth—including that which we need to deal with whatever comes our way, both personally and in the church. If by faith we believed this, there would be a decreased need for Christians to turn to secular psychology.

CHAPTER 13

THE ROLE OF SEVENTH-DAY ADVENTISM

As I learn more about the errors of psychology, I have become more convinced that God has raised the Seventh-day Adventist church for "such a time as this." Through the leading of the Holy Spirit, the pioneers of this church were led to revive many of the truths of God's Word that had been lost over time. These truths are embodied in the teachings of this movement, the Seventh-day Adventist church.

Truths such as the Sabbath, the state of the dead, the sanctuary, the second coming of Christ, the Spirit of Prophecy, the health message, and righteousness by faith are all safeguards that have been given to us by God to protect us against the wiles of Satan. It was God's design that we, as a church and as individuals, would live and preach these truths to lead others to Christ and be changed by His power. Perhaps, if we had been faithful to this charge, we would not have fallen prey to the false philosophies of the world, including that which is found in the discipline of secular psychology.

What are some specific ways in which the truths embodied in Seventh-day Adventism are a safeguard against the errors of psychology? Here are some examples:

1) *The Authority of Scripture:* The Bible admonishes us to "prove all things; hold fast that which is good" (1Thess 5:21). Of the numerous Protestant churches that exist, the truths encompassed in our teachings more closely resemble the spirit of Protestantism than any other church body. This is because our beliefs are so Biblically-based.

In fact, one of the hallmarks of Seventh-day Adventists is that we were known as "people of the book." It is this reliance on Scriptures, *sola Scriptura,* that can protect us from imbibing many of the falsehoods of secular psychology. The importance of depending on God's Word to discern error, such as that which is found in the theories of secular psychology, is elaborated further, as follows:

"…Satan's deceptions will assume new forms. *False theories* clothed with garments of light will be presented to God's people. Thus Satan will try to deceive, if possible, the very elect. Our watchword is to be 'To the law and to the testimony, if they speak not according to this word, it is because there is no light in them.'"[1]

2) *Righteousness by Faith:* Many books have been written (some of which, I must say, are full of truth and others that mix error with truth) on this topic. Thus, I will not get into any detailed explanation of this concept at this time. But I will use the following quotation to explain it in as simple a manner as possible:

"The repentant sinner enters (a) state of righteousness when by faith he accepts it as God's gracious gift. It was through faith that Abraham attained to righteousness (Rom. 4:3, 20–23). He was ready to receive with joy whatever God might reveal to him as duty, and to do gladly whatever God should direct….It was obedience on Christ's part to the righteous requirements of the law that made it possible to declare 'righteous' those who come to Him by faith (Romans 5:6–19). By virtue of this right relationship which the Christian enters into, he is enabled to bear the 'fruits of righteousness' (Phil. 1:11). However, the righteous life that follows…does not earn merit with God… (But)…. A faith unaccompanied by the 'works' that faith produces is 'dead,' being alone (James 2:17).[2]

I have come to learn that this teaching of faith in Christ and His righteousness is a powerful one that the enemy has worked hard to prevent us from understanding. If this teaching were fully understood and practiced, Seventh-day Adventists, and for that matter all Christians, would not turn to secular psychologists for many of the problems that exist on a personal and corporate (church) level.

We would recognize that as finite, mortal humans we have no power to resolve these difficulties on our own. There is no amount of therapy, workshops, books based on secular psychology that can effectively help us. It is only as we exercise a living, active faith in Christ that He will give us the power to cope with our problems. Remember, Paul tells us that we can do "all things through Christ which strengtheneth us" (Phil. 4:13.)

3) *The Sanctuary Message*: The doctrine of the sanctuary is another powerful truth embodied in Seventh-day Adventism that, if understood, would guard us from turning to secular psychology. This teaching helps us to know more about the true character of God, the nature of sin, and how God deals with sin.

If we had a fuller understanding of this doctrine—the price that Christ, the antitypical Lamb, paid for our sins, the investigative judgment, the need for God's character to be vindicated before the universe—many of the earthly concerns that cause worry, sadness, and other emotional difficulties, would pale in comparison. We would spend less time focusing on raising our self-esteem, making sure our needs are met, running from emotional pain and suffering, and more time on contemplating sin, its impact in our lives, and our need to submit to God. This would allow Him to help us to be "overcomers" and better reflect His character to the world and the universe.

4) *The Spirit of Prophecy:* A strong belief in the Spirit of Prophecy—God's messages of instruction, warning, and encouragement through His true prophets—is another cornerstone of the Seventh-day Adventist message. As a church, Seventh-day Adventists believe that this gift of prophecy was manifested through the life and writings of Ellen G. White.

The information given to us through Mrs. White's books provide more guidance and counsel than can ever be offered by the philosophies of secular psychology. The Holy Spirit has revealed to her sound principles that can be used to practically address most, if not all, of the issues we face in the church and in our lives.

Some of the books within which such information can be found are as follows:

Adventist Home—for marriage, family, and parenting issues
Child Guidance—for parenting concerns
Messages to Young People—for issues facing the youth
Testimonies on Sexual Behavior, Adultery and Divorce—for marriage and sexual concerns
Mind, Character & Personality—for emotional and mental issues
Testimonies to the Church, Vols. 1–9—for church and personal concerns
Evangelism—for true principles of church growth.

There are also numerous other books written by E. G. White that address a broad range of subjects. These writings include information about the history of God's church from the beginning to the end of time, the life of Christ, and the Christian experience. Such books, if coupled with the study of the Bible, can provide spiritual strength to those who read them.

In my work as a counselor, I have utilized information from many of these books to help my clients. To cite one example, I dealt with a woman who was suffering emotionally because she was born out of wedlock and felt ostracized and ignored by her mother and her half-siblings. The Holy Spirit impressed me to share with her one page from the book *Desire of Ages* that talked about Christ's life as a child and what he experienced because he was labeled as "illegitimate." After reading this, the woman told me that learning more about Christ's life strengthened her and helped her to realize that she no longer needs to allow her birth status to affect her life. If I had used the traditional talk therapy, we would have spent several sessions talking about how her childhood affected her, without helping her reach true resolution of her concerns. What a waste of time and money that would have been! As I read more of the Spirit of Prophecy, I have become increasingly certain that the information in these books, coupled with the truths of the Bible, can address every single emotional, mental, or social issue that comes our way.*

*Please know that I do not believe that all psychological disorders can be treated by only reading and understanding the Bible and the Spirit of Prophecy. As mentioned earlier in this book, there are some serious mental illnesses that may also require professional medical help.

One final aspect of the Spirit of Prophecy that I would like to mention is the light given through the servant of the Lord on the health message. Many of the concepts of health revealed to Mrs. White by inspiration are, in principle, found in the Bible. However, the Holy Spirit used her to expound on these concepts and help us understand more clearly how we can apply them to our lives.

Recently, science has begun to "catch up" with what the Spirit of Prophecy has revealed long ago about the impact of lifestyle habits, such as how we eat, sleep, and exercise, on our mental health. Many individuals suffer from emotional disorders, such as depression or anxiety, because they do not properly care for their bodies, and this can have a direct impact on their minds. An understanding of this principle is important, especially for some well-meaning Christians who are "anti-psychology" and "pro-Bible," but fail to realize that many people suffering from emotional difficulties or disorders need to learn how to change their lifestyle (sometimes with the aid of a health professional) in order for their minds to function more effectively.

As I have learned more about this principle, I have been applying it in my work with my clients. For example, in the treatment of depression and anxiety, I regularly utilize the eight laws of health, which focus on nutrition, exercise, water, sunshine, temperance, air, rest, and trust in God. As might be expected, not everyone is open to this approach. In fact, I have lost quite a few patients who are not interested in changing their lifestyles and prefer traditional talk therapy, which I no longer do. For those who have been willing to try this method, the results have been impressive.

I believe that if we as Seventh-day Adventists had taken this message of health more seriously, secular psychologists and other health professionals would have been coming to us to learn more about how they can better treat emotional and mental disorders. And we as a church and as individuals would have been much less likely to seek them for help!

There are many other examples of how the teachings of the Seventh-day Adventist church can be a safeguard against the deceptive philosophies of the enemy. In spite of the fact that we have not been as diligent as we could have been (as a church and as individuals) in applying and sharing these teachings, I believe that there is still hope.

God has always had a people, a remnant, who are willing to be led by Him. Such individuals are constantly seeking truth, and as God opens their eyes, they will see error for what it is and rid themselves of its influence in their lives. In turn, these people will be emissaries for Him, "a royal priesthood, an holy nation, a peculiar people; that (we) should show forth the praises of Him who hath called you out of darkness into his marvelous light" (1 Peter 2:9).

Secular Psychology and The Great Controversy

Before ending this chapter, I felt it important to include some thoughts about the potential role of secular psychology in the controversy between Christ and Satan, which began in heaven and continues to this day. It has been Satan's goal to portray God as unjust and unfair to the universe and to win as many followers as possible to his side. And it has been God's goal (so to speak) to reveal His true character of love, mercy, grace, truth, and justice. Many are not aware that one of the critical battlefields upon which this conflict occurs is in our minds.

Simply put, the decisions we make will determine whose side of the battle we will choose—Christ's or Satan's. God has given us His Word to help renew our minds in order that we can, with His help, side with Him in this great conflict. But the enemy has developed a "counterfeit"—secular psychology—to detract us from utilizing the methods God has given to strengthen our minds. It is important that we as Christians understand this danger and make decisions that will ally us with God and not with the enemy. One such decision may be to avoid imbibing the false teachings of secular psychology in our personal lives and as a church. Something to think about!

Secular Psychology and The Last Days

The controversy between good and evil (Christ and Satan) will reach a climax right before Christ returns. During the final moments of this earth's history, there will be some serious decisions that each person will have to make. Upon whom will we depend at this time? Consider the following:

> "Now, if we get in the habit of having men solve our problems, what will be built in our characters? Dependence on whom? On man. And the devil has set every agency in operation to get us into that place, my dear friends, where whatever our problem is, whether it's a financial problem, a health problem, an *emotional* problem, a happiness problem, a religious problem, whatever it is, that there's some man or combination of men that can solve it for us…"[3]

If we develop the habit of looking to man for solutions, especially when we face the chaos of the end times, what will we do? Those who understand the prophecies of the Bible know that in the near future, leaders from both the secular and religious worlds will implement plans that are in direct conflict with God's Word. If we have trained ourselves to look to man for guidance, what will we decide? When we are told how and when we should worship, to whom will we look for help?

I shudder to think of the consequences for God's professed people who have mistakenly placed man's wisdom above His wisdom. However, I also know that He has a people who, by faith, are developing the habit of looking to Him and His Word for guidance (as opposed to secular psychology and other forms of worldly wisdom).

Where do you, dear reader, stand on this issue? Let us each examine our own hearts and our own lives concerning this matter.

CHAPTER 14

CLOSING THOUGHTS

It is my prayer that what you have read in this book will provoke you to re-examine your perspective on secular psychology as it relates to your life as a Christian. The teachings of secular psychology point us to one object—self. This is completely contrary to God's desire for us to be focused on Him.

Sadly, the enemy has deceived many of us about this self-centered emphasis and has led us to believe that we need the philosophies of secular psychology in our lives. But Paul admonishes us to "Beware lest any man spoil you through *philosophy* and vain *deceit*, after the tradition of men, after the rudiments of the world, and not after Christ" (Col. 2:8).

Remember, "we wrestle not against flesh and blood, but against principalities, against powers, against the rulers of the darkness of this world, against spiritual wickedness in high places" (Eph. 6:12). On our own, we are no match for the enemy. His deceptions are so cunning that "if it were possible," the "very elect" would be deceived (Matthew 24:24). It is only through the power of God, through His Holy Spirit, and through His inspired Word, that our eyes can be fully opened to discern his crafty wiles—especially his strategy of mixing truth with error.

We must follow the admonition given in Ephesians 6: 10, 11, 13–19:

> "Finally, my brethren, be strong in the Lord, and in the power of his might. Put on the whole armour of God, that ye may be able to stand against the wiles of the devil... Wherefore take unto you the whole armour of God, that ye may be able to withstand in the evil day, and having done all, to stand. Stand therefore, having your loins girt about with truth, and having on the breastplace of righteousness; And your feet shod with the preparation of the gospel of peace; Above all, taking the shield of faith, wherewith ye shall be able to quench all the fiery darts of the wicked. And take the helmet of salvation, and the sword of the Spirit, which is the word of God: Praying always with all

prayer and supplication in the Spirit, and watching thereunto with all perseverance and supplication for all saints."

It is only as we put on God's armor—truth, righteousness, the gospel of peace, faith, salvation, the sword of the Spirit, prayer in the Spirit—that we can "stand against the wiles" of the enemy. We must clothe ourselves with the armor of God and not the vain philosophies and wisdom of this world.

We must also know that we cannot serve God and Satan—either we follow God's way as we face difficulties and problems in this life, or we follow the ways of the enemy. Thus, I end with the statement that Joshua made to the children of Israel right before his death:

"And if it seem evil unto you to serve the Lord, choose you this day whom ye will serve…"

And may our response be as his:

"As for me and my house, we will serve the Lord" (Josh. 24:15).

BIBLIOGRAPHY

Chapter 1:

1. White, E.G. *Evangelism,* p. 589.

Chapter 2:

1. *Wikipedia, The Free Encyclopedia.*
   Available at http://en.wikipedia.org/w/index.php?title=
   Definition_of_philosophy&oldid=80910201.

2. Watson, Robert. *The Great Psychologists.* (1978). New York: Harper
   & Row Publishers, Inc., p. 146.

3. Ibid, p. 170.

4. Allen, L. & Santrock, J. *Psychology: The Contexts of Behavior.*
   (1993). Dubuque, Iowa: Wm. C. Brown Communications, Inc., p.
   5.

Chapter 3:

1. Bobgan, M & Bobgan, D. *James Dobson's Gospel of Self-Esteem
   and Psychology.* (1998). Santa Barbara, CA: EastGate Publishers,
   Inc, p. 68.

2. Allen, L. & Santrock, J. *Psychology: The Contexts of Behavior.*
   (1993). Dubuque, Iowa: Wm. C. Brown Communications, Inc., p.
   375.

3. Brickman, Chuck. *Maslow's Theory of Hierarchical Needs—Alive
   and Well in the Classroom.* Available at http://teachers.net/gazette/
   JAN03/brickman.html.

4. Sommers, C. & Satel, Sally. *One Nation Under Therapy.* (2005).
   New York, NY: St. Martin's Press, p, 60.

Chapter 4:

1. Abraham Maslow in Edward Hoffman, *The Right To Be Human: A Biography of Abraham Maslow.* (1988). Los Angeles: Jeremy P. Tarcher, p. 207.

2. Holifield, E. B. (1983). *A History of Pastoral Care in America: From Salvation to Self-Realization.* Nashville: Abingdon Press, p. 231.

3. Bobgan, M. and Bogan, D. *Psychological Savior.* Available at http://www.psychoheresy-aware.org/dobsonps72.html.

Chapter 5:

1. Charles Stanley as quoted in Martin and Deidre Bogan's, *An Innocent Inner Child.* Available at http://www.psychoheresy-aware.org/innerc63.html.

2. White, E.G. *Mind, Character, & Personality,* Vol. 2, p. 760.

3. Loftus, Elizabeth. (1980). *Memory: Surprising New Insights into How We Remember and Why We Forget.* Reading, MA: Addison-Wesley Publishing Company, p. 37.

Chapter 6:

1. Kilpatrick, W. *The Emperor's New Clothes: The Naked Truth about the New Psychology.* (1985). Westchester, ILL: Crossway Books.

2. Taken from *"Forgiveness and Self-Esteem.* Sabbath School Lesson Quarterly, April 21, 2003.

3. Lucarini, D. *Why I Left the Contemporary Christian Music Movement.* (2002). Webster, New York, p. 56.

4. Ibid, p. 56.

5. Koranteng-Pipim, S. Adapted quote from *Signs and Wonders* sermon series. American Cassette Ministries. Harrisburg, Pennsylvania.

6. *Seventh-day Adventist Bible Commentary*, Vol. 5, p. 435.

7. White, E.G. *Our High Calling.* p. 184.

8. White, E.G. *Special Testimonies for Ministers and Workers,* No. 8 (7).

9. White, E.G. *God's Amazing Grace*, p. 175.

10. White, E.G. *Review & Herald*, March 27, 1883.

11. Study by Jennifer Crocker, Ph.D. as cited in Dittmann, M. Self-esteem that's based on external sources has mental health consequences…(2002). *Monitor on Psychology.* p. 16.

12. Ibid, p. 16.

13. Mecca, A., Smelser, N., and Vasconcellos, J. eds. (1989). *The Social Importance of Self-Esteem.* Berkeley: University of California Press.)

14. Baumeister, R.F., Boden, J.M., and Smart, L. (1996). Relation of threatened egotism to violence and aggression: the dark side of high self-esteem. *Psychological Review,* 103, 5–33.

Chapter 7:

1. Lucarini, D. p. 40.

2. Ibid, p.41

3. Ibid, p. 41

4. White, E.G. *Selected Messages*, Vol. 3, p. 155.

5. Bobgan, M. and Bobgan. D. *Unconditional Love and Acceptance.* Available at http://www.psychoheresy-aware.org./unconlovl.html.

6. Paulsen, Kevin. *Only of Half Grace.* Available at http://www. greatcontroversy.org/reportandreview/pau-yancey.php3.

7. Bobgan, M. and Bobgan. D. *Unconditional Love and Acceptance.*

8. *Seventh-day Adventist Commentary*, Vol. 5, p. 354.

9. White, E.G. *Manuscript Releases*, Vol. 18, p. 150.

Chapter 8:

1. Brethren Revival Fellowship. Problems Related to Seeker Sensitive Worship. Available at http://www.brfwitness.org/Articles/1994v29n6.html.

2. Warren, Rick. *The Purpose Driven Church*, p. 285.

3. White, E.G. *Second Advent Review and Sabbath Herald,* May 30, 1871.

4. Bobgan, M. & Bobgan, D. *James Dobson's Gospel of Self-Esteem and Psychology.* (1998). Santa Barbara, CA: EastGate Publishers, Inc, p. 63.

5. Bobgan, M. & Bobgan, p. 61

6. White, E.G. *The Ellen G. White 1888 Materials,* p. 844.

7. Walters, Tony. (1985). *Need: The New Religion.* Downers Grove, ILL: Intervarsity Press, p. 5.

8. Brethren Revival Fellowship. Problems Related to Seeker Sensitive Worship. Available at http://www.brfwitness.org/Articles/1994v29n6.html.

Chapter 9:

1. Cole, Steve. Psychoheresy Awareness Ministries: Questions and Answers. Available from http://www.psychoheresyaware.org/questions.html#feeling.

2. White, E.G. *God's Amazing Grace,* p. 109.

3. White, E.G. *In Heavenly Places*, p.131.

4. Schneider, R., et al. (1986). Anger and anxiety in borderline hypertension. *Psychosomatic Medicine*, 41, 242–248

5. Carson, J., et al. (2005). Forgiveness and chronic low back pain: A preliminary study examining the relationship of forgiveness to pain, anger, and psychological distress. *The Journal of Pain*, 6, 84–91.

6. John, E., et al. Anger and heart disease in the Caerphilly study. (1999). *Psychosomatic Medicine*, 61, 446–453.

7. *Seventh-day Adventist Bible Commentary*, Vol. 6, p. 1027.

8. From *The Courage to Heal* by Ellen Bass & Laura Davis as quoted in *Adventists Affirm*. Summer 2003. Berrien Springs, Michigan: *Adventists Affirm*, p.43

9. Ibid, p. 43.

10. White, E.G. *In Heavenly Places,* p. 107.

11. Berkowitz, L. The case for bottling up rage. (1973). *Psychology Today,* July 1973, p. 31.

12. Tarvis, C. Anger Diffused. (1982). *Psychology Today,* p. 33.

13. Holloway, J. Advances in anger management. (March 2003). *Monitor on Psychology,* 34 (3).

14. Jeannette, D. *Living a guilt free life into your life.* Available at http://www.byregion.net/articles-healers/guiltfree.html.

15. Dyer, W. *Your Erroneous Zones.* (1995). New York, NY: Avon Books.

16. Menninger, K. *Whatever Became Of Sin.* (1973). New York, NY: Hawthorn Books, p. 14.

Chapter 10:

1. The American Heritage Dictionary, 4th Edition. (2003). Boston, MA: Houghton-Mifflin Company.

2. Standish, C. & Standish, R. *God's Solution For Depression, Guilt and Mental Illness.* (2002). Rapidan, VA: Hartland Publications, 81.

3. Adapted from Koranteng-Pipim, S. *Patience in the Midst of Trials & Afflictions.* (2003). Ann Arbor, MI: Berean Books.

4. Allen, L. & Santrock. J. *Psychology: The Contexts of Behavior.* (1993). Dubuque, Iowa: Wm. C. Brown Communications, Inc., p. 8.

5. Rimm, D. & Masters, J. *Behavior Therapy.* (1979). New York, NY: Academic Press, p.1.

6. Dineen, T. *Manufacturing Victims.* (1998). Quebec, Canada: Robert Davies Multimedia Publishing, Inc., p.13.

7. Ibid, p. 12

8. Dawes, R. *House of Cards: Psychology & Psychotherapy Built On Myth.* (1994). New York, NY: The Free Press.

9. Sommers, C.H. & Satel, Sally. (2005). *One Nation Under Therapy: How the Helping Culture is Eroding Self-Reliance.* New York, NY: St. Martin's Press.

10. Salerno, Steve. (2005). *SHAM: How the Self-Help Movement Made America Helpless.* New York, NY: Crown Publishers.

Chapter 11

1. Bobgan, M. *The End of Christian Psychology.* Available from http://www.pamweb.org/endofcp.html.

2. Cole, Steve. Psychoheresy Awareness Ministries: Questions and Answers. Available from http://www.psychoheresy-aware.org/questions.html#counseling.

3. Maxwell, Meryvn. Jesus, the True Psychologist. (Summer 2003) *Adventists Affirm.* Berrien Springs, Michigan: Adventists Affirm, p. 11

Chapter 12:

1. *Seventh-day Adventist Bible Commentary,* Vol. 7, p. 342.

2. White, E.G. *Desire of Ages*, p. 827.
3. White, E.G. *Christ Object Lessons*, p. 120.

4. White, E.G. *Mind, Character & Personality,* Vol. 1, p.10.

Chapter 13

1. White, E. *Advent Review and Sabbath Herald.* October 13, 1904.

2. *Seventh-day Adventist Bible Dictionary,* p. 918, 919.

3. Frazee, W.D. *Another Ark to Build.* (1979). Harrisville, New Hampshire: Mountain, Missionary Press, p. 7.

We'd love to have you download our catalog of titles we publish at:

www.TEACHServices.com

or write or email us your thoughts, reactions, or criticism about this or any other book we publish at:

TEACH Services, Inc.
254 Donovan Road
Brushton, NY 12916

info@TEACHServices.com

or you may call us at:

518/358-3494